TABLE SCRAPS
and Other Essays

TABLE SCRAPS
and Other Essays

Juyanne James

foreword by Randy Bates

RESOURCE *Publications* • Eugene, Oregon

TABLE SCRAPS AND OTHER ESSAYS

Copyright © 2019 Juyanne James. All rights reserved. Except for brief quotations in critical publications or reviews, no part of this book may be reproduced in any manner without prior written permission from the publisher. Write: Permissions, Wipf and Stock Publishers, 199 W. 8th Ave., Suite 3, Eugene, OR 97401.

Resource Publications
An Imprint of Wipf and Stock Publishers
199 W. 8th Ave., Suite 3
Eugene, OR 97401

www.wipfandstock.com

PAPERBACK ISBN: 978-1-7252-5173-1
HARDCOVER ISBN: 978-1-7252-5174-8
EBOOK ISBN: 978-1-7252-5175-5

Manufactured in the U.S.A.   NOVEMBER 21, 2019

"Chain of Fools," words and music by DON COVAY Copyright © 1967 (Renewed) PRONTO MUSIC, INC., FOURTEENTH HOUR MUSIC, INC. and SPRING TIME MUSIC All rights administered by PRONTO MUSIC, INC. All rights reserved. Used by Permission of ALFRED MUSIC

To my mother and father, to my sister Willie Vern, to Mrs. Leola (Daughter) Briggs, to Mrs. Dorothy B. Cornist, to Mrs. Verdia Hart, to Dorothy Mae Buckley—all of whom have passed on from this life but remain a constancy in my memories.

I have determined four stages to life:

childhood, where innocence reigns even if at times it must persist;
becoming an adult, when life is most carelessly and most candidly lived;
middle age, when one comes to understand the cruelties embedded in life;
and old age, of which I cannot yet speak, but of which I think I will enjoy, mostly
because I expect to have learned the true value of patience, sacrifice, and love.

Contents

Foreword by Randy Bates | ix
Preface | xi
Acknowledgements | xv

Table Scraps | 1
Sweet Tea | 9
"Chain of Fools," or Aretha Sings My Blues Away | 12
Sugar Cane | 18
The Other Mother | 20
My Brother Went Down | 25
On Becoming a Naturalist | 30
Big Sally and Mitch | 35
Pieces of a Tree | 39
Coming Home | 47
The Guardian | 53
Old Man Carves an Ax Handle | 57
Willie Vern | 59
The River | 69
Momma | 75
Counting Children | 85
Daddy, It's Your Child Song | 91

The Chicken Hawk | 98
Living Spaces | 108
As Fortunes Go | 114
A Daughter Remembers . . . Her Father | 120
The Woodpecker | 133

*Reader's Guide and Discussion Questions
for* Table Scraps and Other Essays | 137
Bibliography | 141

Foreword

"... the sunny fields ... greener as they sloped ..."

The voice of Juyanne James's unassuming prose gently and immediately draws readers into a consciousness that is wise and ageless, a consciousness shaped in her rural youth in the largely African American community of Sunny Hill, Louisiana. There, she lived the necessity of demanding physical labor and near-adult responsibilities within a large, hard-working, and minimally rewarded, but loving family. The consciousness that guides readers through these unforgettable essays is acutely knowing in its sure grasp of human goodness as well as human foibles, and worse. James's is a consciousness and character that—in keeping with the Christian ethics of her upbringing—is ultimately modest and supremely forgiving. Part of her gift is the opposite of the oblivious "innocence" of privileged white people that, in "My Dungeon Shook," James Baldwin warned his young nephew about—before alerting him that he also would have to love such innocents if he and they were to survive and prosper within and beyond the crucible of the Civil Rights Movement.

Juyanne James's very different innocence is grounded in demands and responsibilities that lead to early maturity and in her openness to all people despite her realist's discernment of nuanced flaws among us. She writes indelibly of her work as a child caretaker of elderly white neighbors; of her strong, giving mother, as her guiding light; of her small school's best teachers and mentors being forced to move away because of school integration; of her siblings, especially her sweet-spirited, older half-sister whose young life was marred first by her stepfather's advances, and later by a protracted, disfiguring and fatal disease; and of her dramatically imperfect father toward whom she feels both loyalty and hurt—and, beyond all, love.

These essays speak only fleetingly of their author's rich experience as an athlete, Navy yeoman, professional eighteen-wheel truck driver, trainer of other drivers, professor, and writer. But in a grueling adult summer, clearing acres of a wealthy neighbor's overgrown land alongside her aging father, her re-creation of that experience shines especial. Here, her country-reared, "ferocious" love of the trees and the land and its creatures that she and her father tend become one with the loved spirit of family and a place where "the sunny fields looked even greener as they sloped . . ."[1]

This is an important collection, complexly felt, deeply understood, beautifully written, and always judicious.

—Randy Bates
   New Orleans, Louisiana
   September 8, 2019

---

1. James, "Daddy It's Your Child Song," 120.

Preface

*D*enouement.
 I believe that a writer is largely appreciated because of those who came before her. Yet, it is up to every writer to erect new and vital forms within the ever-growing process of creating literature. For this reason, I have had great difficulty placing this work into a specific category. Yes, I could say these are essays, nonfiction and written from the deepest core of my heart, but all other means of defining this collection may not apply.

 I could also say that these words have come through the course of my mother's and father's lives, though entwined in mine, but that would only be a small piece of truth as well. The essays are separate yet connected. At times, they may not read like essays at all—personal or otherwise—but I have begun to think of them as such, even though I have made every effort to test the limits of writing essays. In this way, and like other memoir writing of today's generation, they break many of the experimental boundaries that define nonfiction.

 The essays also speak to me about the time and place where I grew up—the forever-rustic Sunny Hill—and about the particular love my mother and father shared, for each other and for their children. The essays speak to me about an individual community, where people are always sympathetic and helpful, believing simply and wholly in the overwhelming power of God. And these essays speak to me about who I am and of my realization that the pain of losing my mother was not to be averted, nor denied. The essays tell me that beyond any doubt my mother was a person who knew how to help people, no matter who they were. She still speaks

PREFACE

to me about being an individual and about enjoying my precious time on earth.

The essays also speak to me about my young life, where I learned that we should live each moment and not expect another to take its place. Often, we say things and do not always know the meaning of the words that come, even if very often those words form on our lips so easily. Words like "love" and "forgiveness" come to mean so much more than any abstract definition we could apply. I know that sometimes we must simply live "by the word" because little else will suffice.

When I sat down to write something beautiful, I did not know what it would be, or that it would *be* at all. I have always been aware of my head people, real or imagined, who, like bit players, have remained hidden off stage, waiting for a chance to play to an adoring crowd. Many of these essays come from the incipient ideas of writing a thesis at the University of New Orleans. Even then, I felt excited about setting my real life characters free on the page. It was not until I had spent an entire summer at my childhood home (Sunny Hill) that I began to understand the scope of this work. All summer, my father and I did manual labor together—sometimes in silence after he had fallen into an uncharacteristic pensiveness—and I would feel my people walking about in my head, with their darting eyes, as though they were waiting for a moment to break free. Indeed, I wanted to offer them freedom, much as I do the other real and fictional characters that are stilling waiting, on me, to let them go. These stories make up my life, my dear life, and until now, they have been wasting away.

There were so many people waiting and wanting to be heard as I wrote this work of nonfiction. I instinctively knew that I had to listen to what those voices were saying. I heard my mother say, "Don't be mean to your daddy." I then knew this project could not simply be an indictment against him for all the mistakes he made in his life. I would have to acknowledge the man that he had wanted to become his entire life. If there was a lesson to be garnered from offering my father's story, I surmised that it could not be personal, but instead universal in its message.

I heard my father, the storyteller, say, repeatedly, "Hurry up and tell my story"—a story that would no doubt embarrass the average man. For him, it would confirm to the world that he was a man who came to understand redemption.

PREFACE

I heard my mother and many of her stories, for she, too, was a great storyteller. I often thought her abilities had come through the generations—from the griots of Africa, down through her mother, who passed them on to her daughter. Somewhere along the way, they had found any and every opportunity to testify about the Lord. Not everyone has the gift, really. I believe it comes from being an effective communicator, from absolutely loving to speak, and from wanting to talk out words that might find somebody else's ears.

I heard my sister, Venesta, who, although we are only a year apart in age, rarely remembers our past with the exact same memories. We share so much—good and bad—so I made every effort to blend her life stories with mine. It was her voice more so than my other, younger siblings' (the oldest siblings have now passed on to the next life) because growing up, it was she and I who knew our parents during those rough, unsteady years.

I heard many of the writers I have come to love, from Robert Frost to Toni Morrison to Alice Walker. I heard Plato say, "[W]hen a beautiful soul harmonizes with a beautiful form, and the two are cast in one mould, that will be the fairest of sights to him who has an eye to see it."[1] I heard James Baldwin say something about artists upsetting a type of peace that society tends to take for granted. Usually, the truth is more disturbing than the lies we intimate to the world. In writing these essays, I asked, whose peace will I disrupt in writing my truth?

I also saw many lessons to be learned from those writers, and more. In nonfiction, especially, there is rarely just one story that wants to be told. Nonfiction should not be told from one particular point of view, even if it is memoir. Like life, a writer's apparent truths must converge with everyone else's in that setting if the work is to be accepted and valued. During my writing process, I found that my story had to seek harmony with my mother's and father's stories, as well as with the essence of the Sunny Hill community. Over the years, our family spent as much time in various church services as we did at home, for example. There is so much more to say about the indelible place where I grew up.

I might end by saying something about the reality of my father's awkward devotion to my mother, especially during the later years of their lives as husband and wife. I know that my father loved my mother, even down to

---

1. Plato, *The Republic*, 381 BC.

the neck bones of her, and that he craved her brightness as if it were his life-sustaining power. He relied on her innate sense of taking our family in the right direction. Yet, during those early years, he became her life-stripper, gathering up and carrying off much of her happiness, taking it out of the door of the house with him, and then never bringing it back. Even though I later spent an entire summer with my father, becoming closer to him than I had been in my life, I still questioned many of the choices he made early in his marriage. Very often forgiveness does not give in kind. My mother's words.

Somewhere within the course of writing these essays, I remembered that my father was quite a man. And maybe this is when others began to speak to me as well (teachers, writers, pastors, friends, siblings, coworkers), for this was the first time I was able to draw on a set of conclusions that were there all along, simply waiting for me to see and hear. The essay, "Daddy, It's Your Child Song," though written first, became more appropriately the end, or at least a *denouement* to the collection.

Every other essay became a means to an end, and I was only able to stop writing when "Table Scraps," which was one of the last to be written, became the obvious choice of the first to be read. Subsequently, I went to Louisville, Kentucky, where I received an MFA in Writing from Spalding University. There I worked on the essays that came after the catastrophic event called Katrina. These were the latter days of my father's life, when I found myself writing about the time he and I shared (with me driving him to his doctors' visits and taking care of him in those last dirty days of letting him go).

In the end, I see that the collection found its own way, its own course. I need not have questioned the motives of these real-life characters in telling me, and you the readers, their stories.

Acknowledgements

Special thanks to the University of New Orleans English Department, especially Randy Bates, who as my thesis director mentored my emerging thirst for writing essays, and helped me begin the process of writing about my mother's death. Thanks to his continued friendship and for including me in a writing group that feeds and sustains my craft. Thanks to all the members that group, especially Barry, who is the kindest person alive, and Nordette, who continues to amaze me with her undeniable talent. Thank you Laura, Andrea, Mary, and Sheila for being such outstanding workshop buddies.

Special thanks to Spalding University's MFA program, and all the writers and instructors who embraced me after Katrina, and with the help of Richard Goodman, another mentor and friend, who helped me finish the collection. Thanks (in memory) to Gretchen Tremoulet, who read many of the essays with a most discerning ear.

Thanks to my sister Venesta, who, throughout our lives, has been supportive and who has frankly been an excellent sibling. Thanks to my younger siblings, as well as my nieces and nephews, for being so supportive. Thanks to my extended family of aunts, uncles, cousins, and friends who made my growing up years overwhelmingly special. Thanks to members of the Sunny Hill community, some of whom gave me the confidence to write these essays—I do not think there is a more generous group of individuals.

Lastly, thanks to the University of Holy Cross, where I have worked for many years, surrounded by caring, intelligent people who help make the world a much better place, especially for spiritual and individual growth.

ACKNOWLEDGEMENTS

"Table Scraps" first appeared in *Bayou Magazine* (Issue 60, Fall 2013); "Table Scraps" was also a Notable Essay of 2013, *Best American Essays* (2014); and "The Woodpecker" first appeared in *Ponder Review* Volume 2, Issue 1, Spring 2018.

Table Scraps

In those early days, we never thought about our innocence; we just lived it. My mother was a big part of everything; actually, she was the most important part. She led us and taught each of us, equally. She always had some saying or another, some tidbit of information that we could wrap ourselves in, to use as protection against whatever might come. She used to say, for example, "Keep living," and we understood that she knew what she was talking about: she used these words as though she had personally seen retribution turn around and head straight for anyone who might have harmed her. When she said this, her eyes were their most honest, and yet a wry smile would turn up on the left side of her mouth. My mother surely knew that people who willingly harmed others would never manage to escape this life without inviting harm to themselves, even if one of the people she was talking about sat in the very room with us.

Sometimes I think that when my mother said, "Keep living," what she really meant was to always be in awe of this great world that we live in, and that if we allow ourselves, there would always be wonder and amazement, even through the trials of life. "Just keep living," she would say, "and things will always balance out in the end."

Big black women, they scare people sometimes. My mother scared her share. She got into the habit of running certain unwelcomed people from our house, our first house in Sunny Hill. One day, a police officer came by, claiming that our neighbor's cow had gotten into our field and that my parents "had better" return it. My mother stood in the doorway at this first house, where most of us children spent our formative years, where we worked a dairy business that was not our own, and where we children were sent out on early mornings during the summers to work picking one of the white farmers' crops. She stood holding the screen door wide open, her eyes never leaving the peace officer. He was young and thin, his uniform still searching for his frame. *He is the law*—we children thought to ourselves—*and yet, he stands near the gate, not even attempting to come up the steps and onto the porch.* He almost had to yell to my mother.

"The cow ain't here." My mother told him this several times before she sent my brother for my father's rifle. The officer then rushed to his car and drove off, leaving dust to settle on the situation. But we knew this kind of thing didn't happen everywhere or all the time—this was a small-town, back-in-the-boonies kind of police officer who knew my mother as an honorable person. And in knowing my mother, he knew that whatever she said, she meant. No questions were to be asked, and certainly not the same question over and over. And it always seems to me that in those days people understood how to respect each other and the true concept of right and wrong.

I can still feel my mother's thick, generous hands push me out the front door on those summer mornings when we would be sent out to work. My mother always awakened me with the others—Lionel, Willie, and Venesta, all of whom were older than I was—though we were never certain "the work man" would allow me to go. I'm sure I was six or seven at the time, but I didn't truly start growing until much later—when I turned thirteen. My mother always said it was because I had had pneumonia and measles when I was a baby. "You barely survived," she'd say. But on those summer mornings when we were hired out to work, my tiny frame must have appeared strange to the white farmers, who, although generally interested in hiring as many people as possible to pick their crops, even they had limits. Apparently, I was that limit.

I see the four of us standing outside the house, just beyond the gate, waiting for the man to get out of his truck (sometimes) and the culling process to begin. There was no looking at teeth, or squeezing of arms and legs to find the proper muscles, but he did inspect us with his eyes, staring us up and down and back again.

"Get on the truck," he'd say to my brother. Immediately afterwards, my sister Venesta, tall and lanky, yet only a year older than me, would be told to climb on the truck. "You, too," the man would say, and I knew he was talking to my oldest sister, Willie. They never lingered when they saw Willie either; everyone knew that she worked as though she'd taken work-inducing drugs. She moved up and down those rows of cucumbers, beans, peas, turnips, or whatever else we were picking, at almost twice the speed of everyone else. Sometimes Willie could bargain with the farmers and convince them to take me along, saying, "She won't be no bother, I'll make up her row." Sometimes they just didn't want to be troubled, and I would be sent back into the house, tears not quite falling until I reached my mother. Although she would pull my head to her thigh and tell me to stop crying, she could never sooth the hopeless regret I felt, all because I felt I had somehow let my family down. I would then spend the day helping my mother cook or clean, and if we had no other work to do, we would help my father with the farm labor.

My mother used to say, "If you sing before breakfast, you'll cry before dinner." That early morning hour was reverenced—a time to recognize the Lord's business, to commune with your loved ones, or to do whatever, but it was never a time to sing. Apparently singing that early in the day could be considered a slap in the Lord's face, for he hadn't the time to reveal to us just what kind of day he wanted us to have. For similar reasons, we couldn't sing at the dinner table, girls couldn't whistle, and, particularly, no one could iron on Sunday. So if we were caught doing these types of things, we got "looked" at. My mother's knowing, penetrating eyes would then virtually send us to an embarrassing hole that we couldn't get out of until she finally looked away. None of us wanted to get that look because we knew the look was our fair warning, and that after the look would come her retribution.

We were generally well-behaved children, if that's possible. If she were driving the car, loaded with us kids, there weren't many wild and disruptive fights in the back seat or noise so loud that it would interrupt my mother's driving. And if there was, after several warnings she would say, "I'm gonna give you a backhand lick," and that ended any further untenable behavior. Over the years, we learned how to listen for the tone of her admonition. I've heard that in the African and Asian languages one word has many, many different meanings, and only by listening to the rising and falling of the syllables can the listener grasp the word's proper meaning. In this way, the listener has to have a good ear. Such was our case. Because my mother was generally a patient woman, she often gave us many chances to change our bad behavior before she chastised us. For instance, we received "the look" when we sat in church and misbehaved. Most other mothers came down from the choir stand or wherever they sat monitoring their child's behavior while still trying to enjoy the church service, then grabbed up their disruptive child and led him or her outside to get a spanking. One look from my mother was the first warning, and if she found it necessary to give us two or three looks during the church service, we knew that even God himself could not swing down from heaven and save us from punishment when we got home.

There were many things that we were never permitted to do, such as talk back to her, which my mother deemed the highest level of disrespect. Once—after we moved to our second house and had planted sugar cane for that year—my brother David, who was fourteen or fifteen at the time, had gotten into a fight with our older brother, Lionel. Because Lionel had won the altercation, David—the most hotheaded among us—stormed into the house to get my father's rifle, all the while threatening to kill Lionel. My mother, sitting quietly on the sofa, said to David, "No, you won't. You'd better get back outside with that mess." And David, in his unfortunate rage, on his way to my mother and father's room—which is where the rifle was kept—yelled to my mother, "You don't tell me what to do!" And we all stopped what we were doing, and waited for my mother to come off that sofa raging herself because even though he was a growing boy and stood as tall as she, we had never heard any child speak to my mother in that way. When my brother came out from my mother and father's room, with my father's gun in his hand, cocking the rifle as he walked, my mother—and this all seemed to happen in one swift moment—reached for a stalk of some of the fattest, juiciest sugar cane we had ever grown, which stood leaning against the wall, swooped down on my brother like she was a mammoth hammer with legs, and whacked him so hard over his head that he was immediately rendered unconscious and his body went crumpling down to the floor. Then my mother went down with my brother, on the floor, and began to comfort him. We all stood around looking at them there on the linoleum floor. Yes, there were certain things you just didn't do, no matter what time of day it was.

There was a time in our young family's life when we seemed superior. In our first house, we ate our meals at a small dining room table just off from the back door. There were four large steps that led out the door to the smooth, well-worn ground beneath. Usually my mother would pour the table scraps out the back door and the dogs, cats, and chickens would converge as though none of them had eaten for days. I often tell people that my mother was a great cook, but they can't truly fathom how immense those words are. When she cooked, she cooked, lavishly and with style; yet, all the meals were practical. When we lived at the first house, I remember the huckleberry (blueberry) pies and the stewed potatoes and the roasted meats. And I remember coffee. My mother would serve my father coffee, but we, as children, couldn't have any. "Coffee makes you black," my father explained to us, and although we feared getting this awful color of black that our father talked about, we all wanted to take a sip of his coffee. Usually, he'd pass one of us his last sip and the rest of us would suffer in silence. We all saved a piece of biscuit just for the possibility. The biscuit was then dropped into the cup until it soaked up all the coffee before we ate the delectable brown mush with a spoon.

There came a time when the Morans[1] moved next door to us. We could look out our bathroom window and see their house through the persimmon and pine trees across a small field that dipped like a hollow. This is the same house that the Tabor woman, my father's mistress, lived in before the Morans came. We knew the Morans had moved in when, one day at dinner, we looked out the back door, which usually stood open and against the refrigerator, and saw three little kids standing on and around the steps, all with snotty noses with dirt mixed in, with one or two fingers in their mouths, looking up at us, there at the dinner table, gorging on the beautiful meal my mother had prepared. We were shocked, almost into putting our forks back onto our plates. On that day, my mother invited them in and fed them, and we watched them practically suck big chunks of food into their little mouths, like we'd seen vacuum cleaners do on television. They didn't speak much. I remember elbows on the table, which made me think of the song I'd learned in first grade: "Head, shoulders, knees and toes, knees and toes." It was like their whole bodies were thrown into eating that food.

We eventually fell in love with the Morans. I even fancied one—Danny—as my little boyfriend. Soon after, things changed for us, at least for me and for the Morans. One day they came and stood around our back door steps, probably drawn by the smell of my mother's cooking, and waited to be invited in, but my father said "No!" His anger jumped out at them as though he had shot them with a weapon. I remember sitting there, looking

---

1. The family names (Morans and Tabors) have been changed for publication purposes.

into my Danny's young eyes, and watching him twiddle his finger inside his mouth like he would eventually find food there. And we—my mother included—implored my father to change his mind, but he did not relent. There was no explaining his meanness on that day. None of us thought then that he might have sought some form of retribution against the Morans for moving into the house where his mistress had been forced to move away from. I could not think of an explanation for my father's treatment of our young neighbors. But he held on to that anger.

"They can eat when we're done," he said. And those words cut me, even as a child, to my core. I didn't eat any more—thinking that I would save my food for Danny—but my father ordered me to eat everything. That same scene was repeated the next day and the next. The Morans didn't seem to care that they were eating our table scraps—I guess they were so hungry that they were happy to be eating anything. But I wondered how they could return every day and take the abuse. Much later, I learned that my mother had started saving some of the best of her food, putting it aside and then dishing it out to them after we all left the table.

On the days when I wasn't allowed to get onto the work truck with my older siblings, I helped my mother cook and take care of my two younger brothers, and in the early afternoons, I often went with my father to the dairy barn. Sometimes my father and I would take the tractor to the backfield and collect manure by throwing it into a metal fertilizer that was connected to the back of the tractor. Sometimes we would ride along the property's fence searching for holes where the cows might escape to some other land. My father placed me behind the steering wheel on these occasions so that he could walk alongside the tractor, picking up piles of manure and throwing them into the fertilizer. I could barely touch the gas and brake, so I stood with my feet at the edges of the pedals, my back leaning against the tractor seat, and my arms wrapped around a steering wheel that was rounder than I was.

Somehow, it worked. I drove the tractor at a slow pace, waiting for my father's instructions to turn right or turn left, to stop or go, or to slow down or speed up. Years later, when I became a professional truck driver and driver trainer, I would tell my students that I could drive so well because I had started driving when I still couldn't reach the gas and brake pedals. None of them believed me. Then I'd tell them about my mother's driving, and they truly wouldn't believe me.

"I come from a long line of great drivers," I'd say. My mother, who had learned to drive when she was still quite young, drove fast, yet steadily and safely. Most days she'd drive while singing one of her favorite church songs, which in turn made her want to clap her hands. So there we'd sit, watching her driving, clapping, and singing along. "You gotta be at ease with it," she'd say. "Don't be afraid of nothing."

Once, we went to work for a strange white farmer—strange at first because we were the only people he picked up that day. We had gone out into this farmer's peanut field, and dug those white pubescent nuts from the ground, sometimes with our hands, peeling the soft dirt away. When we had finished working for the morning, this strange white man who had hired us to work for him, told us to "Come on in the house" and eat lunch with his family. I'm sure my sister Willie, in whose care we were entrusted, thought quickly that this might be a ploy to get us inside and then rape and murder us or some other such sinister plot, so she said to the man, "Thank you sir, but we already got lunch." In those days, we either brought a sandwich from home, or bought potted meat, sardines and crackers, or bologna and bread, and drinks to go around when the work truck stopped at Sunny Hill Grocery Store.

The man was persistent in his offerings to us. "No, no, come on in," he said. "My wife's already prepared the food for y'all. Come on in, now." And Willie eventually capitulated, and we went marching into the strange man's house—strange then because none of the white farmers had ever invited us in to eat with them.

There were no steps but one small one, for the back of the house sat low to the ground, and held a screened porch that led to the kitchen. The man's wife, who was chubby just like our mother and wore an apron dirtied by use just like our mother, came to the door of the kitchen and opened it for us. "Come on in," she said, "I figured y'all was getting hungry by now." And we went on in, slowly. Our eyes traveled around the room a couple of times before she told us to sit our tired bodies down at the table. I remember a picture of Jesus on the wall by the table, but not much else; I probably remember that picture because photographs of Jesus—his long dark hair, that sincere and loving look on his smooth white face—always fascinated me as a child. But mostly, I just got carried along with the moment. My brother Lionel didn't seem to care that we were eating lunch with white folks, strange white folks at that, and he sat down and grabbed at his plate, his hands sort of guarding the plate as though he thought someone would take it. Venesta sat down next, and then Willie and I followed. I don't remember any children, just the man and his wife. They sat down and after he said a long and inspiring grace, she started passing the food around. And although they must have talked to us, I don't remember hearing a word. I sat there half eating, half looking out the door, and half knowing what it felt like to be one of the Morans.

My mother always said, "People will lie *on you* when you're living, and lie *for you* when you're dead." My mother was an amiable woman; she had many friends over her life's journey. There is a portrait of her taken when she was in her early twenties. It always hung in my mother and father's bedroom, just above their bed. At the time the photograph was taken, she had birthed several children already. She looked air brushed—all the colors faded into some ambiguous representation of what they had been. And yet, the portrait is still tantalizing in its aesthetic, pleasing way. Her hair is pushed back in waves of shininess. Her smile is wider and fuller than I remember her in those young days of our family's history; the purely pink lipstick is almost dark against a mouth full of glowing teeth. Her eyes are as open and as happy as ever, a slight powdery glaze covering them. And a pair of red-green-yellow colored ear bobs hangs from her long lobes, almost as though they will fall at any moment. Time did not change the youthful beauty of that picture—my mother remained bright and caring and honestly different. And that's the truth.

Sweet Tea

As usual, you are awakened by the sound of his coughing, and know he will want you to come to him. You get up from the palette of quilts and a pillow that your mother has laid for you on the floor of the living room before she left. Slowly, you walk through the kitchen towards their bedroom. It is dark—the kind of dark you have seen many nights before: you imagine that the trees outside are smiling; they are standing around, fully in love with the darkness. You move carefully, though the direction to their room is clear. They are the Bogeys,[1] one of the two elderly white couples that your family cares for, that either your sister Venesta or you babysit on the nights when your mother cannot be there. The Bogeys have no ages in your memory, and neither do you, except that you are very young and they are both very old.

When you open the door and walk into their room, a thin light from the kitchen follows you and your shadow into the room. You almost stumble, knocked off balance by the tugging feeling at the bottom of your stomach. The room is almost cloudy with the smell of coughing.

You barely see his body, lengthy across his side of the bed. You go to him and attempt to release his legs from beneath one of his wife's. You hear his first sound, "Ahh," like a sweet monster in pain.

After he has stood, he leans on you—his hand wraps around one side of your head so tightly that you can only hear from the other side. Then there is only the two of you marching gently towards the bathroom—you could be friends or soldiers in a war, saving each other from some other bad situation in which you have no choice.

---

1. The family name has been changed for publication purposes.

When you reach the bathroom door, you stop at the precipice and allow him to go on alone. You wait outside, but you are not a patient little person. So, you keep yourself busy. You stare at the wallpaper in the hallway and wonder who chose it. The color is faded and a pattern that you do not wish to decipher. It does not interest you. You wait.

Eventually, you hear the door creaking open, and then he appears, with a hand reaching out for you, needing someone to steady him. After you have helped him get back to the bed, he sits at the edge and says the words that you have waited to hear since you were awakened:

"Would you get me some tea, girl?"

He doesn't have to ask you again—his words aren't even necessary. You have left the room even before he has finished speaking. You speed yourself into the kitchen, then gingerly pull the pitcher of sweet tea from the icebox.

Before your mother left you to care for this couple, she has taken two glasses from the cupboard and set them on the kitchen table. You have to stretch a little, but you manage to pour a full glass of tea for him without wasting any. You then pour just enough to cover the bottom of the second glass—plus a little more—for yourself. You put the pitcher away again, then slowly drink what tea you have poured for yourself. You drink it slowly because you want to savor all of it. And though you don't know why, you think of your pastor at church, who on Sundays during charity offerings, says, "Ye are the salt of the earth; but if the salt have lost his savour, wherewith shall it be salted?"[2] You tip the glass up until every drop has gone into your mouth.

As if he hears your enjoyment and understands your pleasure, he calls to you: "Girl, come on with the tea."

You walk to him, half watching the tea, so that it will not spill, and half watching where you are going. As you give him the glass, he greedily takes it and begins to chuggle the tea as though, at that moment, he is the thirstiest of men alive. He turns the glass up as far as he can, almost forcing the tea into his mouth. He leans his head so far back that you see the liquid flush down his throat.

With every swallow you envy him. You think to yourself that when he is finished, you will go back into the kitchen and get more tea, even though your mother has already instructed you not to do so. She has told you time and time again that tea is bad for you. She has repeatedly reminded you that the tea will make you go to the bathroom too often, that it will keep

---

2. Matthew 5:13, KJV.

you awake, and that besides all this, she does not want you to drink all that sugar.

You walk back to the kitchen with the empty glass, and you think you will not disobey your mother, but the closer you get to the icebox and the waiting pitcher of tea, the less control you have. Before you know it, you have poured yourself a half glass and drunk all of it up.

When you are finished, you place the glass on the table and go back to the palette on the living room floor. You fluff up your pillow and fall fast asleep. You do not have trouble sleeping, and you are only awakened when he calls for you again.

"Chain of Fools,"[1]
or
Aretha Sings My Blues Away

When Aretha sings, the delivery is so pure and achingly exact that like life, the joy comes with all the little stops and starts along the way. "Chain of Fools" has always been one of those felicitous songs that strikes me at my core. Long before John Travolta, the sexy and addictive angel in the movie *Michael*, danced to "Chain of Fools," we (my brothers and sisters and I) danced our own chain, our own fool's dance, just inches away from the newly blacktopped road that ran in front of our first house.

My sister, Venesta, who lacked any rhythm whatsoever, strutted and smashed her bare feet into the hot summer dirt, and I laughed myself into a sweetly wrought hysteria, the same way I smile these days when I think of that long ago moment.

There is a picture of us standing there by the roadside, as though we were famous—the new road acting as indelible proof of our status in life. The picture says even more than I can remember. I only see my brothers Lionel and David, my sisters Willie and Venesta, and myself, but I can feel the presence of one of my parents, my mother, who was probably standing on the front porch, laughing her affecting laugh—the one that rolled from her rather than shot out all stark-like. She might have been standing against the post, the one that we reached for on our way up the thin front steps. She would have been wearing some print cotton dress or another, and it

---

1. Don Covay, "Chain of Fools," 1967.

"CHAIN OF FOOLS," OR ARETHA SINGS MY BLUES AWAY

would have had the smell of fish or chicken or maybe potatoes, or whatever we were having for dinner that day. She always started dinner early, like in the wee hours of the afternoon. We always ate early—maybe because people were always stopping by to eat with us: the preachers, the deacons, our Aunt Josephine, my mother's friends, the neighbors, and whoever else cared to.

My non-official godfather Murley came by as much as anyone did. At some point in our relationship (when I was a toddler), he saved me from an ant bed. "For some strange reason, she just sat there," he would always say as he recalled how I screamed and screamed but never moved until he came for me. He loved me like no man has since, or so they tell me. To him, I was the most beautiful baby that God had ever delivered. So, he came and went and came and went, always bringing something into our lives—sometimes tangible things like candy and drinks for us kids, and sometimes not so tangible things like peace and understanding for our parents. But more than anything, he brought us music.

I can't see Murley's truck, which probably sat under the adolescent oak tree next to our outdoor garage. That tree always seemed desolate to me and older than it actually was—all alone except for the garage, its branches low and barely aging. And I always wondered about the garage. For one thing, we were the only people who seemed to have such a garage; and for another, it was so separated from the house that my father more often parked closer to the house, just beyond the front gate. There was a period of time when we thought the garage was haunted, because my father wouldn't park there. It was just that we children were all tucked in bed, and didn't see him pull close to the fence—so he could use it as a guide and support on those backward, early mornings when he maneuvered his drunkard self into the house.

The music is what attracted us to Murley more than even the honey buns and candy and chips and drinks that he brought us. On that particular day, Aretha's song stepped out of his truck the way he stepped out: very proud and with a chip on its shoulder. The music seemed to bounce off the inside of the truck door, hit us straight in the face, and start a chain reaction, as our bodies began to move.

> *Chain, chain, chain . . . chain, chain, chain . . . chain,*
> *chain, chain, ain, ain, ain, ain, chain of fools . . .*[2]

My sister Willie would have mostly just stood there grinning on the sidelines like she always did. She was so much older than us that our antics probably tickled her as much as they did my mother. My oldest brother Lionel's flat top head articulated his efforts, his dark skin separating him from the rest of our thin, nut brown colored bodies, his heart and his smile probably the same shade of rashness. He snapped his fingers, and once again tried to be the authority on everything, this time on dancing and singing. I'm sure that even the cows in the backfield could hear his off-key sounds.

My sister Venesta danced as little gray dust clouds kept her private company, and my little brother David and I smiled because she had turned us into joyous laughing fools. And somehow I danced myself, even though I was mesmerized by the moment. David followed my movements, for he was my living shadow then. Now, I think that I must have been remembering as well because I am the only one to remember anything about this day: the music being soaked into our soul's feet, the lady on the radio singing as though every note came from her heart's beat—her rhythmic harmony imploring us, warning us about the troubles of being in a chain of fools. All I know is that every time Aretha and her girls sang *chain, chain, chain*, so did we.

> *You got me where you want me;*
> *I ain't nothing but your fool . . .*[3]

I am sure that we clowned our way deeper into my mother's heart that day as she stood there on the blue-gray painted porch, watching us. The porch ran the length of the front of our small house. It was the same porch that was renovated into another bedroom when my cousin Eddie Joe came to live with us, after her mother—my Aunt Josephine—died from a broken neck in an automobile accident. The same porch that stood just high enough off the ground so that on the many and resplendent occasions when my mother allowed us to make homemade ice cream, we could stand on the ground and freely turn the creaming handle of the ice cream machine, until the ice cream got so hard that only the strongest of us—usually my

---

2. Covay, "Chain," 1967.
3. Ibid., "Chain."

brother Lionel—could turn it. My mother, yes, she would have stood there enjoying life and enjoying us, like she cared nothing for the mean world we danced around in. Her laugh would have persevered, a conduit through which these rare moments would have given her respite. Although she has since passed on from this life, it is her laugh that I remember most about her. That cranking, eloquently smooth and guttural laugh had come down through the generations. It was her mother's laugh; it was a laugh that all her sisters shared; and it was a laugh that when I grew to be a woman, would also be mine.

> *You treated me mean,*
> *oh, you treated me cruel . . .*[4]

There was no sadness that day, no crying, except the happy tears that ran down and formed our river of joy. I am saddened to remember now that my father wasn't there. He was probably in town (Kentwood, most likely), pretending to buy feed, or not pretending at all, but rather boldly going about in his world, creating his second little group of dancing fools—the ones we would find out about many years later, the ones who got even less of him than we did. Sometimes he would catch us, his first children—on the outside of the house, next to the living room window or at the back door on the steps—before he left for the day. His credit had gotten so bad that he couldn't open a checking account, and thus, neither could my mother (a fact that deeply distressed her). Perhaps he simply thought that he would acquire more than he was entitled to if he used the little assets he called his children.

"Sign this check for me," he would say. And whoever's name was on the checking account that week, month, or whatever, would print our little names on the blank check, some of us as best we could. Then he'd rush to his truck and drive away. Sometimes we'd jump on the truck's sideboards and try to ride along, but he always saw us and slowed down just enough that we could jump off before he picked up speed again and fully drove away.

---

4. Ibid., "Chain."

I might be weak yeah, but I give you strength . . .[5]

My sister, Venesta, always says that what she appreciates most about our mother is that she talked to us, really talked to us. Not like we were children and certainly not like we were stupid and had no sense. She would tell us everything, and when she did, it was all intimate, like she was letting us in on the rudimentary and/or evil secrets of the world, so that our having heard these things would make us aware, and so that when and if the evil ever showed up on our door step, we would recognize it and send it packing without even a hello, and if that failed, we would knock it down the steps, over and over if it were necessary.

"Your father's gone to see that Tabor woman," she'd tell us again and again. The name Tabor came to sit like dirt in our throats, all gritty and earthy and too filling, and with no redeemable flavor. Sometimes when my father was getting dressed to "go out," we'd ask him if he were on his way "to see that Tabor woman." His just-shaved face would turn away, and he'd tell us to "go outside and play." He never wanted to talk about it the way our mother did.

And yet, I remember all the days and nights when we were riding up and down the road (looking for my father) or were sitting at home and my mother's eyes were looking out the large picture window in the front room, and she would say to us, "He's your father." That's all she had to say, really. The tone with which she said it was everything to us. That tone said your father loves you. It said no matter what, we're all going to get through this. And when my father came home on those days after cashing his milk check (from the diary business we helped run), and he had bags and armfuls of presents for us, we were crazy about him, not only for the presents, but also because he was our father. Because our mother found a way to forgive him, so did we.

Today, I understand that the reason I was eventually able to let go of the bad memories is because of my mother, because she stayed in that debilitating relationship, thinking only of us. I know that the life my father was leading should have torn our family apart. Instead, when I look back on my childhood it seems closer to perfect than spoiled. The same joy that flooded us on that day when we danced and clowned to "Chain of Fools," I carried with me throughout those years. No matter how many times my father came home late, or how many times he fought with my mother, or

---

5. Ibid., "Chain."

how many times he used us to get over on the world, none of it mattered so much in the end. And though the rest of the world may have seen us as an unbreakable chain of real life fools, I can say, without a doubt, that none of us ever thought so.

Sugar Cane

In that small area of Louisiana where I grew up, and where some small farmers still grow sugar cane, the biggest delicacy was to sit around the fire on cool autumn evenings and eat sugar, in its natural form.

Someone, most likely the father (and sometimes an older brother or any woman with strong hands), is designated as the peeler. Everyone else simply sits around the peeler, as closely as possible, so that he or she is certain to get the largest share of the cane booty.

The long stalks are cut in two, leaving the bottom, the sweetest half, for last. The peeler bares his knife (cuts a ring) around the bottom edges of each section of the cane, so that when the knife peels downward, it will stop at that section rather than continue down the entire stalk of cane. There must be, you see, order in the peeling of sugar cane. Exposed cane dries quickly and gets dirtied by the air, leaving a slight distaste in the mouth of the person chewing the cane. A good peeler moves quickly, section by section—the sharp thin knife slicing down the outer edges of the stalk. The purple and green peelings don't fall to the floor but have to be chucked to the side, away from the freshly peeled sections of the cane.

When the section has been stripped of its outer bark, the peeler thrusts the knife down the middle and then makes a perpendicular cut, forming a cross, and leaving four equal sections of the cane. The peeler cuts these sections into one-inch lengths and drops them into a waiting bowl. The little chunks of cane barely hit the bottom of the bowl before little and big hands reach in and grab them up. All that can be heard at this point are the unmistakable sounds of mouths munching, jaws squeezing the living juice out of the cane. The incredible sweetness of the sugar cane waters the mouth; it is a sweet pleasure that can hardly be rivaled . . . until all the juice has been chewed out of the cane piece. It is then discarded, like the outer strips of the cane bark—useless and in the way. All that remains is a dry, white mess that resembles shucks of old battered hair that we would eventually take to the pigs for their chewing pleasure.

The Other Mother

It was late October, we weren't going to the fair, and my mother did not seem to care. She sat resolutely at the dinner table the night before, and as she chewed on her pork salad, she said, "We gotta help your father strip cane this year." I couldn't believe it. The Washington Parish Free Fair had been a yearly tradition in our family since I remembered. When my mother did go to the fair, she situated herself on a bench outside the Exhibitions Building—on the off chance that one of us would get lost and would therefore know where to find her.

But my father loved going to the fair as much as we did, probably more. He would drag us all over the fairgrounds, buying us ice cream, hot dogs, peanuts, and cotton candy. He would let us ride the Ferris wheel and the bumper cars, and late into the evening hours he would lead us back to my mother, carrying the worn-out little ones, with the rest of us trailing at his feet.

Actually, until that warm fall day, we children probably had no idea that we were poor. We probably guessed at it, but never really placed that label on ourselves. With ten children by then, our little family had bubbled over, but my parents always managed to get the things we needed. My father often bragged that he was the only man he knew never to hold down a job. I guess he didn't count the Army—his term as a cook in the Aleutians during World War II wasn't like every other job. Years later, after the children had come along, he would wake up on special mornings and make us all the homemade apple turnovers that we could eat. He would say, "Count your lucky stars 'cause the only thing I make better than this is lima beans." Of course we would grimace at the horrifying possibility of having to eat lima beans. Even our mother didn't cook them, and she cooked as though she had studied with the chefs in heaven's kitchen. She could throw together three or four pans of biscuits long before she heard our feet, one by one, spank the morning floor. She was the only person we knew who could make commodity eggs taste like our hens had sat on them overnight. Sometimes we'd have salmon and eggs (salmon from the can), eggs and gravy, bacon and eggs, and even brain and eggs—which most of us tried to ignore, but couldn't because other than liver and gravy, everything my mother cooked was acceptable to our taste buds.

The thing you should know about my mother is that she always had two separate yet astonishingly equal personalities. My sister Venesta and I had started reading up on astrology, and after we figured out that our mother was a Gemini, we understood—it was the twins. One twin wasn't necessarily bad and the other good, but over the years they had become just that in our minds. We clearly preferred one to the other.

One mother—who we liked to think of as the real mother—was stout yet graceful; when she moved, her entire body smiled. She was the one who sat in the living room on Sunday mornings in her slip and girdle, as she stuffed powder into her bosom and under her arms. Her face always had one pleasant expression or another written across it.

The other mother stood taller, and looked down on us with eyes that could see through any lie we dreamed of telling. This mother had a type of oppressive anger that enveloped us all. The look on her face usually belied some hidden worry or something she needed to fuss about.

We had an old, mean cat that my father had named Stinkybutt, and even he steered clear of the other mother. We could sometimes be frolicking out in the yard and look up to find her eyes chasing us around. Apparently, the real mother simply stored up all our bad behavior, and when the other mother showed up, she doled out punishment like she had found it on sale. We couldn't look at each other in a suspicious way, or accidentally bop someone upside the head, or steal someone's chicken leg while they were reaching for another piece of bread. It was just understood that we would be punished for every little mischievous act we did. And for some quirky reason, the other mother always cooked the dreaded liver and gravy for dinner.

We unconsciously prayed for the real mother to be at the breakfast table every morning. And based on whoever was waiting for us, we knew what type of day we might have. The real mother always had friends stopping over to visit, and she prepared dainty little pimento or egg sandwiches and homemade root beer for everyone. She encouraged us to have our friends and cousins over, and in the summers she would put us to work turning ice cream on our front porch. And when we did things like chase or be chased by someone carrying daddy-longlegs or dead spiders and snakes, she found it entertaining—often bowling over at the waist, her laughter sounding off down through the woods.

Sometimes she would sit outside with us, long after dark, and tell us her life stories. They weren't like the tales my father told us. His were supposedly adventures he had lived through while traveling in the Army. Like the time he was chased by mosquitoes that were bigger than the average man was, and he only managed to escape by darting behind a tree at the last moment. Apparently, the mosquito's giant beak went straight through the tree, and while it was stuck there, my father ran to get his hammer and bent back both sides of the long beak, leaving the mosquito a permanent part of the tree. We laughed at my father's aberrations, but we sat in awe of my mother's realities.

My mother deferred to my father and would only tell us her stories after we pleaded. Mostly, we wanted to know about the café that she worked at when she lived in Baton Rouge: "Mama, tell us about the time you made biscuits for Elvis Presley." Even in the darkness of the early evening we could see the satisfying smile on her face as she told it once more: "He came right back there in the kitchen where I was and said, 'Ma'am, them was some of the best catheads I ever had!'"

Whenever she told us about the time she had to walk to work because all the colored people were striking against the buses, we would always suggest some alternate means of transportation for her: "But Mama, why didn't you and Daddy just buy you a car?" or "Mama, how come your boss man didn't come pick you up?" She would laugh hard, probably at our innocent little minds.

Sometimes the other mother told us sad stories. She would tell us about her and our father's first child, Anna, who died before she was a year old. But we would inevitably ask so many questions that my mother would get angry and start searching for work that we could do. The other mother seemed to spend most of her time punishing us. Not once did we stop to think that she may have been carrying heavy burdens that she could not share with us.

On that morning that we weren't going to the fair, I was certain that we would be eating liver before our heads found our pillows that night. The other mother was gathering us up like soldiers and sending us off to the cane field. She had just stepped out the back door to check our progress when we heard the unmistakable sound that tires made when they slid to a stop on our gravel driveway. My mother shooed us on, telling us to hurry, and then she turned to go and meet our visitor. She could have been her own vehicle the way she walked, at an accelerated rate, like she was switching gears as she went.

A man in a white shirt and pants, and black cowboy boots had gotten out of his truck and was leaning on the front of the hood with some papers tucked under his folded arms. My mother stopped at the edge of the porch and crossed her arms, leaning her robust frame on one of her skinny legs. The two of them (our mother and the man) could have had a shoot-out if they had been armed. Instead of doing what we were told, my older sister and I had quietly followed my mother's steps until we were within earshot of her and the man in white.

My mother was the first to speak. "I don't know what you're doing here. I told them people yesterday we'll pay the Light Bill when we get some money."

For some strange reason the man took my mother's statement as an invitation to come closer. Walking towards her, his boots made munching sounds as they dug into the gravel.

"I understand that, Mrs. . . ." He flipped through the papers searching for my mother's last name.

"No need looking at no papers; you ain't cuttin' off our lights," she said. "I got chullin to feed. I don't know where the next meal is coming from, much less money for a light bill."

"I understand that, Mrs. James." The man had put a name to the angry face that stood before him. "I do, Ma'am, I do understand, but . . . well, I'm just here to do my job. They tell me to come out and cut you off, I have to come out and cut you off." And with that, he raised his shoulders and lifted his arms in the air; his palms opened to the morning sun.

His apparent lack of concern for our predicament must have ignited an already flickering flame within my mother because before I knew it she had reached down and picked up my father's favorite fly swatter from where it lay on the porch. Though we were behind her, I knew her eyes were glaring at the man when she brought the dead-fly-ridden swatter up and pointed it at him. Her large arm shook back and forth like it was getting revved up. Then in a voice that we kids had come to think of as the voice that could welcome souls to hell, she said, "YOU AINT CUTTIN' OFF THESE LIGHTS, I ALREADY TOLD YOU THAT!"

But you had to be there to see the fear that swelled up in the man's eyes. In all the years that my mother had scared me and my brothers and sisters senseless with just a simple look, we rarely saw her work her intimidating magic on an adult. It was like magic that she was standing there telling the Light Bill Man what he could not do. Without saying another word, the man opened the door of his truck, got in, and made his getaway. My sister and I watched as he made it to the end of the road. But as the taillights of his truck flashed quickly and he turned onto the main highway, I felt my mother's eyes land steadily upon us.

"What are y'all doing?" she yelled. "I told you to get down there and help your father!" My sister and I fled as well, but as I walked along the muddy path that led to the cane field, I couldn't stop thinking about what had just happened. My mother had saved our electricity with a few desperate words and a fly swatter. I suddenly felt as though I didn't know her at all. The other mother had used her anger in a way that I had never seen before. It was the first time since I could remember that my mother was no longer two distinct personalities that I could either love or hate, she was just my mother.

I looked back just in time to see her step inside the house. I didn't see her again until lunchtime when she showed up with commodity cheese sandwiches and homemade root beer. She called us over to her, gathering us around her like a hen does her baby chicks.

We didn't make it to the fair that year, but I learned that some things were more important. I can still see my family down in the cane field that day. We all chopped down cane with my father. We stripped it and we stacked it; and we delivered it to my uncle's syrup mill. And not once did we complain.

My Brother Went Down

I remember being six or seven-years-old, and our family was going to the one of many baptisms at the creek where our church carried out its baptisms. I was apprehensive about standing near bodies of water because once, when we were down at the pond near our house, my brother Lionel had pretended to throw me in. He grabbed me by the seat of my pants and the back of my shirt, and swung me back and forth. I was so afraid that my body stretched out rigidly, anticipating each swing as my last. Finally, he grew tired of his game, and allowed me to fall onto the red clay edge of the pond. I sat there for a moment with my legs buried beneath me. The warmth of the ground was soothing—a few blades of grass shot up between my legs. But I hated my brother in those days. And it would be a long time before I was able to go near the pond again. On that day, when we were going to the baptism, the fear still hadn't left me. It played in my mind like a song that just would not end.

    We drove up to the creek, and my father slowed down as he searched for a place to park. As we passed by, I peered around my sister's head, which was pressed to the backseat window. I could see a small group of people making their way down to the baptism ceremony. A heavy-set woman whose hair looked like shiny waves were running through it almost slipped down the little hill that she was descending. One of the deacons, who walked next to her, grabbed her arm just in time. My sister Venesta laughed her seesaw laugh. My mother, in the front seat of our car, said something about laughing at the Lord's business. After we found a place to park, we made our way back over the bridge. Looking down as we crossed it, I saw that the ceremony had already begun. There were people dressed like colorful soldiers lined up along the bank of the creek.

They were singing, almost moaning, "*Come let us go down to Jordan, come let us go down to Jordan, my Lord.*"[1]

When my mother started down the embankment, she held on to my father's shoulder and sort of shuffled down the grassy hill. I thought of our milk cows when they went sliding down the slippery slopes of the pond. Lionel made a large leap and was down the hill before the rest of us. Venesta and I slid down in our black patent-leather shoes. Little brother David followed. The singing stopped, and I heard our pastor say something about going down an old person and coming up a new one.

Stepping over the protruding roots of overhanging trees and into the sandy footprints of the people who came before us, we eventually found an open space from which we could see the service. We stood attentively facing the pastor, who was standing in water that came up to his thighs. Against his white robe, the water was black like the smut in our chimney. As he spoke, the curled hair above his lips moved up and down. I smile now, remembering that Venesta always said he looked like a walrus.

"As Baptists, we believe that the body must be immersed in the water," the walrus said.

"Amen," a chorus of people of agreed.

"By confession of their faith, these men, women, boys, and girls, have chosen the Lord Almighty." This, the pastor said with his arms stretched out to a group of people huddled close by and dressed in white sheets. Some of them nodded in agreement; some bowed their heads. I saw a little boy with hair smashed to his head. He was new to our church and didn't look much older than I was. He stood there glaring at his bare feet. I wondered if he really wanted to be there.

The pastor continued: "When you go under the streams of this running water, your soul will be washed clean."

"Amen," the crowd answered.

Stretching out his right hand, the pastor said, "Let me have the first one who will come. . . ."

Our tallest and leanest deacon gently parted the benign waters with his large feet, then turned and faced the huddled group. A young woman stepped out first; her face said she was related to the little boy. The deacon took her hand, leading her to where the pastor was standing.

---

1. Anonymous, "Let Us Go Down to Jordan."

As she waded through the water, the chorus of people began to sing: *"My sister went down and she didn't get lost; she didn't get lost; she didn't get lost. My sister went down and she didn't get lost, religion so sweet."*[2]

This sister took her place between the two men, and the process began—the same process would be repeated over and over until the last of the group was baptized. The pastor placed her crossed hands over her chest, and covered them with his large right hand. Then he placed his left hand behind her back, and before he could finish saying, "I baptize you in the name of the Father, and the Son, and the Holy Ghost," he had forced the woman to fall backward into the water. For a few moments she lay stretched out like I had seen dead people at funerals. She seemed to give in, as her body became a floating testament of trust and obedience.

My own body went numb. I wasn't aware that I was holding my breath, but I must have been because when the woman came up, I felt my heart beating again. To me, the water that streamed down the woman's face was like the sheet of ice I'd seen on puddles. She looked frozen beneath it. The pastor wiped her face with a towel that hung over his shoulder and then gently sent her wading back to her group.

As she struggled to make her way out of the water, the chorus of colors sang again: *"My sister went down and she didn't get lost . . . ,"*[3] only this time, everyone sang the words with smiles on their faces. I found myself singing happily along. I was glad that the sister went down and didn't get lost.

When the time came for the little boy to go down, I cringed. And almost as if he felt my fear and was feeding off it, his dead eyes met mine and stayed there until the deacon took his hand.

> *"My brother went down and he didn't get lost; he didn't get lost; he didn't get lost. My brother went down and he didn't get lost, religion so sweet."*[4]

Both men came closer to the edge, but the water still came up to the boy's chest. His eyes darted about, perhaps looking for me, perhaps reacting to our shared apprehension. The pastor said something that I couldn't hear, and the boy tried to smile, but I could tell it was one of those fake smiles he felt obliged to give.

---

2. Ibid., "Jordan."
3. Ibid., "Jordan."
4. Ibid., "Jordan."

Because I was so frightened for the boy, I couldn't watch him go down. I leaned my head back. For the first time, I noticed that the trees that stood over me had put on their last coat of green leaves—little flakes of sunlight fell through them and landed on my face. The warmth from the sunlight washed over me just slightly, softly, like a morning's breeze. I tried to see beyond the tops of the trees—to catch a passing bird or a cloud, or anything that might take me away from the hard cold surface at the water's edge. I heard the splash of the boy's body entering the water and waited for the jubilant singing.

In my dreams, on many of the nights that followed the baptism, this little boy never came up. He floated downstream beneath a bridge with his arms crossed over his chest and the tips of his toes sticking out of the water like snake eyes. And I stood on the bank of the creek looking on, unable to move or make a sound. It was one of many recurrent nightmares I had as a child.

But in reality, I leaned forward again, I heard the chorus singing: *"He didn't get lost; he didn't get lost,"*[5] and I felt my heart beating once more. As the boy climbed out of the water, his eyes found mine again. He looked shiny new like grass and trees after it rains; I no longer wondered if it was fear that clouded his eyes.

My brother Lionel—the second oldest, always the most courageous, and the one that had grabbed me by the seat of my pants and pretended to throw me into the pond when I was a child—would later die at 41 years of life. Because Lionel had rarely owned a car during his life, he had walked the small roads and highways of Sunny Hill to get to where he wanted to go. Late one Friday night, as he walked home from a party, he crossed over a small bridge—much like the one in my dreams—and was struck by a passing vehicle. His body was dragged for over a hundred feet, and was barely recognizable when my father and I showed up at the funeral home to make the arrangements.

My brother and I had never gotten close, and not because he spent so much of my young life tormenting me—after all, as kids we all seemed to torment each other. Over the years, our lives had simply run different courses. I became a professional, and finished college; whereas, he remained on a course of odd jobs and borrowing money to get by. And yet, he was the

---

5. Ibid., "Jordan."

one who had maintained a lengthy relationship—a common law marriage to a woman named Ethel Mae for over twenty years.

My dreams of a young boy floating downstream ended years later. Nowadays, when I cross the bridge of that old creek where our church used to have baptisms, I think about that particular baptism and I think about my brother.

On Becoming a Naturalist

In the presence of nature, a wild delight runs through the man, in spite of real sorrows. Nature says,—he is my creature, and maugre [despite] all his impertinent griefs, he shall be glad with me. Not the sun or the summer alone, but every hour and season yields its tribute of delight; for every hour and change corresponds to and authorizes a different state of the mind, from breathless noon to grimmest midnight. Nature is a setting that fits equally well a comic or a mourning piece."[1]

—RALPH WALDO EMERSON

Howard Gardner proposes that we have a multiplicity of intelligences, one of which is the naturalist.[2] I have often thought of intelligence and how we come about it, but mostly what I've wondered is how I came about my potential as someone who loves nature. When Gardner uses the term, I think he means someone who could be an expert at biology or even

1. Emerson, *Nature*, 1836.
2. Gardner, "The Theory of Multiple Intelligences," 2006.

someone like me who just loves nature. The naturalist simply has more of a connection to the outdoors than other people.

Looking back, to my days as a growing toddler, I know that I had a most inquiring mind, and that I was naturally attracted to the outdoors. If I were placed on a pallet (of quilts) on the floor of the living room, I usually found my way to the opened door and would pull myself up on the screen door and stand there, legs wobbly as I struggled to remain standing, peering out into the front yard—at least this is what my mother told me many years later. She also said that if the screen door wasn't locked, I would push my way through and crawl out onto the porch and sit there, generally, satisfied with myself, just happy to be out of doors.

But much of this behavior was exhibited before I learned to walk at eight months old. It would seem unlikely to me that this is true except that as I grew older, as a toddler, I remember being outdoors or wanting to be outdoors all the time. And after I'd made it outside, the lawn became an expansive play pen for me. I once walked over to a large brown mound of dirt and sat on it, but was quickly rescued as I've said before, by a loving godfather because I had sat in an ant bed. I sat there until he came for me, crying out until I was whisked away to safety. My mother said she gave up on trying to stop me and often moved my pallet to the grassy front lawn as I got older. It apparently no longer suited me to remain on the porch. I wanted to linger in the grass, searching out bugs and other crawling insects, watching them maneuver their way up and around the sturdy stems of grass and twigs.

Many of my most ardent childhood memories are of animals and insects that I discovered as a child. I once grew so fascinated with a woodpecker that had been searching out insects on a light post near our house that I could hardly sleep wanting to watch the black bird with the tip of red on its head peck on the post. The years passed, but I still remember that it was only the spiders and daddy longlegs that frightened me away from my father's tool shed. Actually, I didn't care much for the earthworms that converged on our backyard after a hard rain. I can see clearly all the cicada shells that I found on the sides of trees. I remember all the fish we caught with our child-made hooks and poles when we went fishing. I remember the skunk that my little brother David chased behind some old stacks of lumber without getting skunk spray all over him (much to my mother's joy and astonishment after we told her about it). And I remember all the redbirds, bluebirds, and sparrows that I chased around our yard, running and leaping as though I were some nimble-footed cat bent on getting my prey.

Were it not for these early escapades with nature, I would have to determine that my family was the true instigator of my dedicated love of nature. We did, after all, first live on a dairy farm and later, just a farm. And we did, after all, spend more time out of doors than in, it seems. In the early days, after the cows had been milked, I helped my father spread manure and grass seedlings over the pastures until I became old enough, for sure, to go with my older siblings to pick vegetables for the neighboring white farmers. When our family was forced to move away from the dairy farm, we ended up at my dead aunt's homestead. This, I believe, is where my potential as a naturalist was truly nourished, in good and bad ways.

For one thing, there on the farm was a thing that we affectionately referred to as "going down the lane," which really meant that someone, like my brothers, was headed into the woods, usually to find my father's mule, Jake, or our pony, Mitch, or to find lost or stranded calves or cows or goats that we hadn't seen in a while. The lane, a path about the width of a one-lane road with fenced in fields on both sides, ran for about a hundred yards before it drifted into a gentle opening and then into full-blown acres of woods. Only my father and my brothers were generally allowed beyond the lane. Often, they took my father's rifle and went hunting, as men were *supposed* to do. My mother repeatedly said that there was nothing but trees, brush, and animals in the woods and tried desperately to convince the rest of us, my sisters and me, how dangerous the woods were. She spoke of black bears and bobcats, not to mention snakes, such as copper-headed moccasins and deathly corals. I kept the rhyme in my head: "Red next to yellow and he's a friendly fellow, but red next to black, step back, Jack!" Armed with this information, I felt capable of making the right decision if I saw such a snake. Just next door to where we lived, one of my cousins had almost picked up a coral snake before an older child had saved her from that awful fate. Frankly, I felt confident, competent, and safe in the natural world of the woods.

It now seems amazing that I made my way into these very woods that my mother had warned me about, and on every occasion that I could successfully do so without detection. When everyone else was either in the house or busy in the front of the house, I would sneak my way down the lane—sometimes not so sneakily, I would playfully hang on the fencerow as I went, gently tickling my heart with the imaginative thoughts that went through my mind. Sometimes I would sing songs that I'd made up or talk to the people who became part of the adventures I created in my mind.

When I made it to the wooded area, I would at times stare up at the tall trees. Some of them I fell in love with over the years, awed at their mighty strength, pushing out the other, weaker trees with their desire to grow so tall and bountiful. Sometimes I'd sit at the base of a young live oak or pin oak tree and listen to every sound that came to me. The birds calling each other became familiar sounds that I cherished. I tried to mock them and call them to me, wanting more than anything to have my favorite, a redbird, a cardinal, sit on a neighboring limb for a spell before it flittered away again. I learned to watch for and to notice the quietness of nature. The woods were a place where the animals reigned, but they knew how to be silent when I needed them to be. This stillness of nature is what I came to truly love, and nothing could frighten me away from it.

Another of the reasons why the distant woods were so fascinating to me was because back at my house, the world seemed to be a turning force against me—as though nature had gone awry and created some unnatural wonder called our family. Usually, there was no such thing as a peaceful moment. The natural course of events included the constant fighting with my siblings, who seemed charged by my quiet nature and who became fueled into action by it. Most days, my brothers and sister, Venesta, chased me with dead (or living) spiders and daddy longlegs (the things that did frighten me). Around and around the house I ran, and back through the house seeking out my mother's protection. Venesta, whom I have grown to appreciate, was my nemesis then. Although we were constantly together, forced by both the proximity of our ages and my mother's unyielding idea that we should be treated like twins, we generally hated the sight of the other and would strike up a fistfight at a moment's notice. So, I learned to steal away from this unpleasant home of ours and to look for my serenity elsewhere.

As the days and years passed, it wasn't just my siblings that I wanted to get away from. As I got older, I learned to look out for my older sister, Willie, for we all knew she wasn't of full mind and that she thought of life in playful terms, no matter what happened to her. When I had been almost a teenager, I had a friend who loved me greatly. She followed me around and held on to our moments together as though they were precious to her. She never wanted to leave me to go back to her own house, and when I went to her house, we both struggled to keep me from going back to mine. She would often play with my hair, wanting to comb it and re-braid it, because my "good" hair was long and pretty and hers was not. She also thought I was better than she was simply because my skin was brighter than hers. When I would go to my friend's house, she and I would at times sit in the living room and watch television, but soon enough one of her brothers would find us there and he would begin to harass me, trying to run his hands up my skirt or shorts or whatever I was wearing at the time. My friend would make herself ready for my rescue and help me fight her brother off. Soon enough, we'd both have our knees dug into his body, punching him as hard as we could. These beatings never stopped him from trying to feel me up, and we never stopped beating him up. When I think of it now, I realize I was learning a skill that I needed to have.

On many of those journeys down the lane, the people in my made up stories would disappear and I would hear real voices—the voices of my father and my half-sister, Willie. I would hear her giggling and then say to him, "Quit, you. You better quit," as she squirmed not so hard to get away from my father. And I would hear him dismiss her words, and I would sometimes see him when I came quickly on the back porch and find him with his hands rifling all over her, touching her in places that I knew no father should touch a child, even though she was a young woman by then. I knew she didn't really want to get away from him, but I also knew he was behaving in a way that suggested he was not moral. It was a game they both played, only she didn't know any better. But rather than deal with it, rather than confront them there at the scene, rather than run to my mother, when she came home, and insist that she hit him once again and try to beat some sense into him—rather than do any of these things, I would try to hang around as witness, and try to protect Willie. More often I found myself walking down the lane and into the woods—woods that my mother had assured me were dangerous, woods where all manner of dangerous animals purportedly lived, even sat in waiting for young girls like me to devour. It wasn't that I didn't believe my mother; it's just that the real danger seemed to lurk closer at home.

Perhaps, as I said, my love of nature was nurtured by my family's dedicated effort to remain so close to the land. Perhaps it was cultivated and fed by all the unnatural things I heard and witnessed during my growing years. Life is like all those trips down the lane—no matter how much uncertainty lay beyond, the value of each trip was in the peace I collected just being there.

Big Sally and Mitch

If you should find yourself at Girls Scouts Camp—at the beautifully sprawling 400-plus-acre Camp Marydale, where you have been made Assistant Camp Director for the summer—and the Director of the Riding Staff has challenged you and two of your prankster buddies to a race, all because you have showered her bed with pepper and other seasoning ingredients and taken her spare sheets and tied them in a line across the roadway that leads to her bungalow, then you will accept this challenge and go directly to the stables to pick out the two horses that will lead you to victory the next day;

And when you arrive at the open spaces of the large sunny field behind Shady Haven and see that all the campers, from Tanglewood to Owl's Roost, have come to witness this event, you will smile to yourself because you know that you are your own secret weapon, for you are young and impetuous and not afraid of anything, but mostly because you have the rare combination of having been raised on a farm where you have learned to ride every imaginable type of moving vehicle, including horses who attempted to run at the speed of sound, oblivious and unresponsive to whomever was riding on their backs;

And when both teams have assembled with their horses and agreed on the race rules—that each team must travel a distance from the starting line to an ostensibly low hanging oak tree that stands alone in the middle of the field, allowing each of the three teammates one trip down and back, and that the winner will be the team that crosses the finish line first, having used both horses—you will gather your teammates together and persuade them to ride harder and faster than they ever have because you do not intend to lose this race, even though your opponents, as the horse-riding experts, are favored to win;

And when you designate yourself as the strongest rider on your team, and as such you will ride the last and most likely determining leg of the race, you will do so because you will know the legitimacy of this label and your ability to pull it off, for you will think momentarily of the first horse that you rode—a mare that your father named Big Sally, apparently because there was a small Sally somewhere—a horse so tall that all of you except your sister Venesta could walk under its belly without bending your heads and without disturbing even one of the long hairs that gathered at the belly's center;

And you will also think of Mitch, the pony that your parents bought for your brother Lionel's tenth birthday, and of how, after Lionel had allowed you to share a ride with him but then later disembarked and left you to sit on Mitch's bare back with nothing to hold on to but the short end of his mane, your younger brother David, out of jealousy or pure devilment, had thrown a rock at the usually docile pony, causing it to bolt and run through a small space between two trees—an action which separated you from Mitch's back as though you were cream that needed to be cleared from the top of aging milk—;

And you will watch the appointed race and cheer and plead with your teammates to hurry and to ride, ride, ride, and surprisingly, your second team member will cross the relay line only seconds behind her opposing team member, and you will lean down so close to your horse's neck that you will have to look to the side of the horse's head to see where you are going, and your legs, though they are encased in the straps of a saddle, will hug the horse's belly and your heels will dig sharply and abruptly, so that the horse will take off running so fast that had you not been holding on, you would have fallen off;

And you will look just beyond you and see your challenger and feel the after draft of her horse's motions, and though your heels are kicking at your horse's sides, imploring it to run even faster, you will then find it necessary to hold on to the horse's rein with your left hand as you begin to slap at both sides of the speeding horse with the long end of the rein—left then right, left then right, so that the counter motion of the straps coming down on the horse's body will resemble windshield wipers going back and forth and clearing your path, even though dirt and pieces of grass are flying everywhere;

And when you are almost caught up with your opponent and you see that the oak tree, from which you are to round and then head back in a final rush to the finish line, is just beyond, you laugh a wicked laugh that only you and your horse can hear because you see that your opponent has decided, like every other rider in the race, to go around the low hanging tree instead of under it, and you allow her to do this because you instinctively know that she has never had to ride a horse the way you have—bare backed, because your family could never afford a saddle, and fearless, because after you had fallen off Mitch that first time, you had summoned your courage and gotten back on again—;

And not only this, but your opponent does not know that there have been days in your young life when you have ridden Mitch, and horses like him, when he did not want to ride you, and he would reach his head around and try to bite you on your legs in an attempt to dethrone you from his back, and if you insisted, he would then buck and canter at so offensive a pace that your bottom would be sore the next day, or that you, your siblings, and all your neighbors have often taken turns riding this cantankerous pony up the road, to the top of the long hill on Highway 450 by Mr. Wince's place;

And that upon turning in the direction of your second house, Mitch will have taken off running so furiously that if, even for a moment, your legs have lost contact with his belly, you will have fallen off, either as he leaned and turned down the dirt road to your house or when he finally reached the back gate, for although you have been screaming as loudly as you can for someone to open the gate, usually everyone has ignored you, and when Mitch has reached the gate, he will have stopped so abruptly and so closely in front of it that even those with the tightest grip will have fallen off and landed on the opposite side;

And because you know all of this, you will continue to laugh your wicked laugh and you will cut under the oak tree, with your head leaning down even past the horse's neck, as you do your best to avoid being knocked onto the ground by the unforgiving branches of the tree, and though it is a battle, you somehow win, you somehow hold on, and you somehow get in front of your opponent, who is just rounding the tree as you have come from under the tree and begun your final dash to the finish line, and you won't bother to look back because you know that now it is your after-draft that she must breathe;

And when your horse comes flying across the finish line first, you will feel as though you have been riding on wings, for the horse will feel light beneath your legs, you will have felt the coolness of an undeterred wind on your face, and you will not feel the heaviness and burden of a loss—everyone's cheers will now have met you because, as the underdog, you will have taken on the appearance and aura of a winner, and in proportions only afforded to legends—and yet, you will walk over to your challenger and not only shake her hand but ask that the score be settled or at least buried until another day.

Pieces of a Tree

I shall not; I shall not be moved.
I shall not; I shall not be moved;
Just like a tree that's planted side the water,
Oh, I shall not be moved.
I'm on my way to glory; I shall not be moved.
I'm on my way to glory; I shall not be moved;
Just like a tree that's planted by the water,
Oh, I shall not be moved.[1]

When I first read Ernest Gaines' story "Just Like a Tree,"[2] about this grand old black woman having been set upon the earth like an immovable tree, I did not love trees as ferociously as I do now; I simply thought favorably on them and hoped they favored me as well. I have been known to sit up under a nice, rounded shade tree and feel really close to God. Although I have always been a naturalist, I had no means of fully

---

1. Anonymous, "I Shall Not Be Moved."
2. Gaines, "Just Like a Tree," 1963.

understanding what Gaines meant in comparing a woman to a tree. My own mother, as well as the many teachers whom I adored, was yet alive. I had not begun to think of her or them in terms of loss or how precious they might have been to our community. I could only relate the impact of Gaines' protagonist to one of my favorite teachers, one who had, over the years, stretched her metaphorical tree branches over the many students she once taught at Vernon School. Vernon was an all-black school that had been forced to close during the desegregation period of my young life.

I believe we have to know about loss before we can understand what it takes from us. I also believe there are things that can be taken from us in this life that have nothing to do with loss. Some things, we naturally lose along the way. And there is no need to place blame; perhaps we can lament the earthly loss, but that's it. This has become an unfortunate truth for me, just like a writer's search for truth—tormenting her, keeping her searching, always trying to figure out what exactly "is" the truth.

Some days I wake up thinking about the often strange relationships we have within a community. I remember being five and six years old, and while the remainder of my family worked in the hot afternoon fields, picking vegetables for market, my sister Venesta and I babysat two old, white couples—one of whom was, for all intents and purposes, our grandparents. At least we children thought so. For years, I believed that these surrogate grandparents could not be trusted to do for themselves: not even to turn on the stove and warm up whatever food my mother had sent for their lunch. I could do that, even at such a young age. I could help them to the bathroom. I could get up and change the channel on the TV. I could pour them glasses of sweet tea and pour myself a little as well. I could even carry on a bit of conversation if they felt like chatting me up.

Over the years, I came to understand that this particular old white couple was not only not my grandparents but that our family actually worked for them: some of us in the fields and some of us, like me, who was too young at that point to pick vegetables, worked in the house, feeding them, helping to clothe and take care of them because their own family members either lived too far away or simply did not care. For all of our work, my family was paid the privilege of living in a small house on their property. It became our first and most precious house—the one we would think about years and years later, after we were forced to move. But the only reason I did not know the particulars of this symbiotic relationship with the old couple was because my mother seemed to want it that way. I am not sure why; perhaps she liked the idea of us kids thinking of the old couple as our kinfolk; perhaps she first loved them and we then loved them, too. I choose to think of it as just our way of loving everybody we could.

Mostly when I think of those days, I think of my mother. It is true that you can keep special people in your heart, store them along with the memories. Some years ago, after I first graduated from college, I would go home to the country and sit on the front porch with my mother, in the late afternoons. We might watch one of our old cows, Sue, as she munched her way along the outskirts of our yard. As we halfheartedly kept track of the cow, my mother and I would carry on conversations big and small, from what she was cooking for dinner to the private schools that had been built over the years since desegregation. This was a topic that rarely left our conversations. We marveled that there was still separation of the races; the only difference was that we had lost our beloved school in the process.

If I said a human body knows how to protect itself instinctively, I believe I could say *that* alone and not have to say anything further on the subject of loss.

I was a little girl wearing print dresses and patent leather shoes to school when Vernon School became one of the first all-black schools in our area to physically separate and join the nearby white schools. This was long after the landmark 1954 court case, *Brown v. Board of Education,* had led to the eventual desegregation of schools in America. After the matter had made the rounds in every public and private court of appeal, our local government decided that the black students at Vernon should be separated and dispersed amongst the various white schools in the area. The idea of white students joining us at Vernon was apparently unthinkable; it simply could not be contemplated. And even though black heads and white heads roiled and thought and debated, trying to figure a way out of this unpleasant predicament, none could be found. The truth is that Vernon School was one of the best schools in the area, and losing it became a long-lasting travesty.

Vernon High, with students from first to twelfth grade, boasted certification of all its teachers and graduated one of the highest rates of students to matriculate into the nearby colleges (in and out of state). Many of the teachers lived in what seemed to us at the time like far away cities: Baton Rouge and New Orleans. Some carpooled every day; some spent their weeks in the Vernon community and their weekends back in the cities. Many of the teachers bought homes in the Vernon area and became influential, industrious members of our community. They joined our churches and became the deacons and deaconesses who sat on our pews and spoke so loudly and properly of God's business—there was never a twang or a slurred syllable; all of their words rolled off their tongues with a certain shapeliness. They shopped at the Cavalier Shoppe or the Boston Store, wearing smart and tactful clothes and smelled of perfumes and colognes. They drove the best and latest models of Cadillacs and Buicks. They patted us children on our heads in approval. They softly rebuked us to "Stop running through the halls!" when we were at school, and to "Respect God's house" when we were in the sanctuary at church. Our parents came to trust these teachers and rely on them for their clear minds and level heads. And perhaps out of a sense of duty, or perhaps to fill that vacant need, over the course of years, these teachers became the great leaders that they were thought to be. They were indeed the guardians of our society; they were at the heart of a community that built itself around them.

On the second Sundays of every month, of every year, the Junior and Sunbeam choirs were appointed to sing. Our ages ranged from the tiniest among us to those proudly proclaiming themselves teenagers. Most of us feared one part of the church service more than we feared the sight of guts, spiders, and snakes: what we feared most was the testimony hour. From the pastor to the deacons and deaconesses to the choir members and all the members of the audience, each person was asked to stand up, before the church—and more importantly, before God—and give their testimony, their 'termination. The aged and wise members of the pulpit and many of the elders of our church would give rousing accounts of how God first saved their souls, or how they had once been saved and then become backsliders before God saw fit to bring them back into the fold. One such testimony might go like this:

"I stand before you today to give my testimony. I was born in the church; my mother and father brought me to church as a child, but when

I became a grown man, I went my separate way. I didn't take to pleasing God then. I was young and foolish. I threw away all my money on women and drink. And I heard the Lord calling me over the years, but I wouldn't listen. I didn't slow down for nobody or no thing. Oh, but the Lord, he got a mighty big hand, and he can reach far and he can reach high and low. Early one morning, he reached down and grabbed me by my ankles and I felt like he turned me upside down. He twisted me and turned me until I didn't know which way was up and which way was down. The Devil had got so far up in me that the Lord had to shake him loose. I was driving in my old Ford, but next thing I know the truck had hit this big ol' tree and was rolling over this way and that. I knew if it rolled one more time, I wasn't long for this world. I called on Jesus. 'Jesus,' I said. 'Jesus.' But the Lord didn't look like he was going to hear me. I called on Him some more. And praise the Lord, he heard my cry. I woke up in the hospital some days later, bandages all over me, with a leg near gone. But the first thing I said was 'Thank you Jesus. Thank you Jesus.' I tell you the Lord can make a way out of no way. He'll pick you up when you're torn down. He'll set your feet on solid ground. And He'll forgive all your sins. But you got to praise Him. You got to live right. When I got up from that hospital bed, I decided to follow Jesus, to live right. I decided to step on board with the Lord. I decided to point my way straight to Heaven. I'm here to tell you today that the Lord is able. It's been ten long years and I ain't turned back. Ten long years and I'm on my way to Glory. Ten long years since I put my hands in Jesus' hands...." Then the entire church would jump in singing,

> *I have decided to follow Jesus;*
> *I have decided to follow Jesus;*
> *No turning back, no turning back.*[3]

When time came for us little people to stand and give our testimony, our music teacher, Mrs. Hart, would promptly lift herself from her seat and act as our leader by giving her testimony. As she got older, or if she wasn't feeling particularly well, she didn't stand up so much as she half stood, her body bent slightly out of a sense of order or decorum. We could hear the first words flow out from her even before she stood up to speak, for she always began by reciting her favorite Bible verse.

"Let the words of my mouth and the meditation of my heart be acceptable in thy sight, O Lord, my strength and my redeemer." This 19th

---

3. Anonymous, "I Have Decided To Follow Jesus."

psalm of David, for our director of music, for this teacher at Vernon School, was always her prelude, her introduction to this long-established occasion. These words rang out from her without fail.

After the Bible verse, she would tell the attentive congregation, "It is my determination to make Heaven my home." She usually made a few other statements about how she planned to live her life in the sight of God, and then she was finished. Each of us, from the smallest to the oldest choir member, would follow her with our own version of what she had said. For those of us who were frightened of speaking out in church, or who simply felt too young to have a 'termination, much less be able to speak of one, we felt justified in repeating her very words.

"I'm determined to make Heaven my home," we would say.

First one then another, we would belt out these words as quickly and effortlessly as we could without sounding as afraid or as embarrassed as we felt in that moment. It wasn't easy. Afterwards, we could relax, our young bodies no longer rigid from the prospect of having to declare ourselves. Then our music teacher would softly run her fingers over the piano notes,

> *Lord, I want to be a Christian, in my heart, in my heart;*
> *Lord, I want to be a Christian, in my heart.*[4]

And we sang along. This part we did not mind because our favorite verse would eventually come:

> *Lord, I want to love everybody, in my heart, in my heart;*
> *Lord, I want to love everybody, in my heart.*[5]

And if it were a particularly moving and spirit-filled day, we would continue until even the least favorite of the verses were sung:

> *Lord, I don't want to be like Judas, in my heart, in my heart;*
> *Lord, I don't want to be like Judas, in my heart.*[6]

We had learned about Judas in our Sunday School lessons, and none of us wanted to be like him.

After Vernon School closed its doors, the school became run down, as did the community. Many of the teachers had to find jobs since most were not

---

4. Anonymous, "Lord, I Want to Be a Christian."
5. Ibid., "Lord."
6. Ibid., "Lord."

hired by the schools we had all been bussed to. Our music teacher was one of those teachers. Over time, the teachers' voices slowly disappeared from our neighborhoods and churches. On rare occasions, our music teacher would travel those roads that she had found so familiar when she was bouncing back and forth between New Orleans and Vernon, and she would visit us at church. As soon as we saw her walk in and find her seat near one of the front pews, our voices would perk up and sing louder, our bodies would stand straighter, and our hearts would beat with a little more purpose. And when the church services were over, we made our way over to bask in the joy that rested with her. When she saw us coming, she would beam loudly, "There's my girls and boys."

Two months after Katrina, after I was allowed back into the city of New Orleans, I set out to see the Lower Ninth Ward—the part of the city that suffered most from Katrina; it was the part of the city where my music teacher, Mrs. Hart, had lived. When I found the house, I saw that it wasn't glaringly different from those surrounding it, but there were sure signs that the person who lived there knew they were special. I marveled that none of us had ever come to New Orleans to visit her over the years. We had only known her as our teacher, in our world.

My eyes saw an old Cadillac; the floodwaters had now thrown it against the front bedroom of the house. In the center of the yard, stood an ornate address post with the numbers 2-9-6-6 hanging, squeaking in the breeze. Beneath this sign, a patch of new green grass was beginning to grow. The hedges held their old trim, but now stood in place like death's quiet sentries, wearing the browned out color of Katrina's destruction. The house resembled paper or cardboard that I could tear down with my bare fingers. Bricks that once blanketed the house now lay in piles of debris on the ground. The front door and all the windows of the house were missing. A fat and stuffy lounge chair sat in the doorway, facing any visitors who would come.

Everything in the house, for as far as I could see, remained layered in a dark, muddy confection, a type of dirt that would linger, I was quite sure, as though it felt welcomed to stay. Everything beneath the layer of mud appeared to be waiting to be taken up and used again. I thought of particular people who place plastic over their sofas to protect them. Looking downward, almost at the floorboards of the outside wall, painted on the white brick, next to the doorway, in large letters, was the date 9/21 and then a large X. At the bottom of the X was a 0, and to the left <sP.

Those numbers meant nothing to me, for by then, I knew that she had been rescued by helicopter but had never made it off the bridge where she and others like her had been stationed, waiting for further transportation, to be moved on to another resting place. Her old heart must have given out, possibly at the thought of being moved again, possibly because she was determined not to be moved, not one more time. I often wonder if there was someone with her in those final moments, someone holding on to my music teacher's hand, telling her that it was okay to finally rest.

These days, I think back on the great women, the great teachers, who influenced my young life. There is no mistake that I feel like one of the most capable, most spiritual, most musical people I know. I know who is responsible for this. I clearly know. Just like the matriarchal figure in Gaines' story, I was blessed to have metaphorically been shaded by some pretty spectacular trees.

Coming Home

After my sister Venesta joined the U.S. Navy, everyone assumed I would join also, and I eventually did. This was not exceptional at the time, except that we were two small town black girls who, other than having played basketball and traveled around the state, generally had not gone beyond the confines of Sunny Hill, Louisiana, but were suddenly traveling all over the world.

Venesta had joined up, gone to boot camp and "A" school, and was then stationed in Naples, Italy. We sent her almost daily letters from home, hoping that she would not be so lonely. I think it was in those letters that Venesta and I grew to be close like true sisters. There I was, the next oldest of us left at home after she signed up for four years of military service. That November, she was transferring from Naples to London and decided she would drive to London in her car. Actually, the plan was for her to drive to London, catch a MAC Flight to New Jersey or Philadelphia, then catch a flight out to San Francisco. I would pick her up there, and we would drive the 2, 300 miles home to Sunny Hill.

After boot camp in Orlando, Florida, and "A" school in Meridian, Mississippi, I was sent to Point Sur, California, for my first duty station. Venesta and I could not have been at more opposite ends of the world. But clearly the miles could not separate us, with our new adventuresome spirits. The first Christmas at Point Sur was miserable (mostly because, as a lowly seaman, I was on duty in the base galley, and was introduced to things like succotash—Lima beans and corn—and Lumpia, both of which I would come to love over the three years I was stationed there). Venesta and

I decided we would not disappoint our mother (nor ourselves) by not going home for the holidays.

After I picked up Venesta at the San Francisco airport, we drove back to base, then loaded my luggage and gifts into my tiny little red Chevy Chevette. One of those gifts was a ten-speed bicycle that we had to literally stuff into the car, even after we'd taken the front wheel off. We began our trip home in the late afternoon, three days before Christmas, sure that we could drive non-stop and be home by Christmas Eve.

I wish I could bore the reader with every detail of that trip. The things I do remember is that we learned just before our journey began that our good family friend, Mrs. Leola Briggs (Mrs. Daughter, to us), who had been diagnosed with breast cancer, was now in the hospital. Having the disease, in those days, usually meant the patient would be terminal, so, even as Venesta and I were pulling away from the base, our hearts were quite heavy. Perhaps that is why we spent so much of our drive lightheartedly looking back over our time in the navy, not to mention having grown up in Sunny Hill.

It was difficult to release Mrs. Daughter from our minds. Why had she spent so much time at our house when we were children? Yes, she was our mother's best friend, but at times it seemed as though she lived with us, she and her son, Cecil. They were like fixtures, even more than our Aunt Josephine before she died. There was the time Mrs. Daughter was sitting on the toilet in the bathroom (of our first house) and had spotted a tree climber (snake) crawling up one of the near trees of our yard. The snake was huge, as we later found out when she shot it down with our father's rifle. As we drove along, Venesta and I remembered two things about that day: Mrs. Daughter's strict rule that snakes and other such creatures should be kept as far as possible from children, and the fact that years later, I continued to have bad dreams about snakes.

Venesta and I laughed about the many times we tortured Cecil (he didn't seem to fit in with us—always wanting our toys and yet never sharing his.) It was on that car trip we realized that perhaps he didn't have any toys, that as a young boy with no father and just Mrs. Daughter for a mother, he was lacking a few things. That did not stop us from laughing about the time Mr. Cat's bulldog bit a plug out of Cecil's leg. We were all running past Mr. Cat's house, trying to avoid the dog, but apparently, Cecil, who seemed fit and capable enough, still couldn't outrun that little fat dog.

Mostly, we remembered how kind Mrs. Daughter was to our mother—that as a friend, she seemed to outrank any others mostly because during the roughest days of her marriage, our mother found an ear and a whole lot of support in Mrs. Daughter.

That first night, somewhere in Arizona, along Highway 10, one of us fell asleep while driving, and ran off the road. To this day, both Venesta and I assume it was the other person who did this. I do remember that the driver remained awake for many hours after the incident (frightened by the thought of driving off one of those ditches that seemed to go down without end); this allowed the other sister to get some sleep—so much so that she was ready to take over the driving duties at first light.

Throughout the day, we listened to music on the radio, carrying on our seat dancing, and hating it when we lost the best radio stations. Every song seemed to take us closer to home. Every time Al Green sang "Love and Happiness," we'd talk about our brother Lionel. "Fire!" by the Ohio Players would come on the radio, and we would laugh and berate him some more. Lionel had somehow gotten our parents to buy him a stereo as a Christmas gift (I'm sure it was for the family, but he claimed the stereo as his own)—it boasted an 8-track and phonograph, encased in a walnut case that was almost as long as the entire living room. It was frankly beautiful, and those speakers put out a sound that was incredible. Our brother boasted all over the community that no one had a stereo like him. He played his music at all hours of the day and night.

Even back then, we questioned where our parents got the money—although they always found a way to get us some of the things we wanted for Christmas. And we (the other siblings) didn't seem to mind because we, too, found our way to the record store when we had a dollar or two saved up and could buy our own favorite records. I joked that the music may have been the only thing that saved me from embarrassment that particular night when every player on the basketball team had been allowed to play except me. It was quite awkward. I mean, we beat the team 103-5, and I still wasn't allowed on the court. I felt so bad that I thought I would die. On another occasion, our second basketball coach had insisted on bringing Venesta and me home from one of our games (instead of allowing us to ride the bus like everyone else). Our parents had not given us permission to ride the bus; we were actually supposed to "catch a ride" with one of our teammates who had a car. When I got home, I played my favorite record, the Three Degrees' amazing hit, "When Will I See You Again," over and over and over. Venesta and I laughed, knowing that Lionel couldn't have been home.

During that trip home, our conversations always drifted back to the navy and all the craziness of boot camp and "A" school. Venesta and I shared similar experiences leaving home: getting on the Kentwood Greyhound bus, all the way to MEPS in New Orleans where we were processed into the military. After being sworn in, about five other enlisteds sat around the airport with me, waiting to catch a flight to Orlando, Florida. I remembered being so excited that I could not eat the food my mother had packed for me (since I left home on Thanksgiving Day before dinner was served). I would later regret not even taking one bite when we finally arrived at our training facility and we were told to take everything we owned and place it in a box, to be shipped back home—ostensibly, the navy would now provide everything we needed.

    We had similar stories about being chosen for the drill team—me, actually on the staff drill team, which meant I was one of five recruits in our unit who would practice our drills as well as perform for graduations. We laughed because both Venesta and I were chosen for the drill team because we were taller than average, had great posture, and an athletic body. At boot camp, we spent most of our time in school (military classes), and we skipped "work week" duties, where the recruits took their turns working in the chow hall or other duties around the base.

    "I had to direct baby booties [new recruits] where they could sit in the chow hall," Venesta said.

    "Well, I guess I wasn't so lucky because we had to wash the laundry for everyone in our training unit," I said.

    "Do you remember when we went to the gas chamber?" she asked.

    "Yes, I hated it. But loved Fire Fighting class."

    "Yeah, that was around the same time we learned to fire guns and got aboard the Blue Jacket [an old navy ship being used for our training]."

    "Yeah, we pretended we were taking the ship out to sea, but never left port."

The more we drove, the more we talked about boot camp. It's where we both truly learned how to pull pranks on others. I remembered a specific night when I just happened to be on compartment watch, and a group of rowdy recruits decided to play pranks on everyone who had gone to bed early. The CC (Company Commander) had given us late lights, which meant taps would sound late that night. While I remained on lookout, the pranksters sewed people's sheets together, sprinkled their beds with baby powder, and even tied one girl to her bunk with dental floss. She woke up and tried to get up but couldn't. They also topped her off with powder. Some people's sheets were taken off and dumped in a neat pile by their rack. Some people's mattresses were thrown into the head (bathroom).

"Yeah," I said, "The DPO [Duty Petty Officer] came out and caught us and told us to stop, but all the while she was laughing her head off. No sooner than she was gone and we were back at it. (By this time, I was off duty and had joined in with the pranking.) Some silly person put Vaseline on all the toilets, and one person actually sat on one of the greased toilets. God, that was funny."

"That night seemed to never end," I said. "It's true. We started putting toothpaste in people's shower clogs. One section leader got out of bed to go to the head and she let out a big yell. There she stood with Crest toothpaste running out of her toes, but she was still laughing. All of us thought we'd never stop laughing. People would wake up and find the toothpaste that we had put in their hands was now all over their faces and in their hair. One of the pranksters finally got tired and wanted to get in bed, but couldn't because her sheets had been shorted. She never skipped a beat, and just jumped over to the next girl's rack. Then someone yelled, 'Hey, Harris, that girl's got crabs,' and Harris couldn't get out of that bed fast enough. By then, we were laughing so hard we could barely move. It was so funny because the other girl didn't have crabs at all."

All along the route home to Sunny Hill, Venesta and I had to stop at phone booths and call our mother. To think of it now, she must have been pretty frightened for us, but kids never think about the worry they put on their parents. Those days of being away from home must have put a lot of gray hair on our mother's head. When we finally pulled up to the house, late Christmas Eve, I understand now why it was our mother who was the happiest to see us. The hug seemed endless. She told us she had been cooking all week for us. Sure enough, there was every kind of cake and pie she had ever dreamed of cooking: cheese, jelly, plain cake, hummingbird, sweet potato pie and egg pies. And of course the dish she had always been known for, chicken pie (a form of chicken and dumplings that is the most savory thing one can eat). The table was full to bursting over. And after we ate, the family sat around the dinner table, and thereabouts, full and happy to be together once again.

It was perhaps that joy that we took with us when everyone piled in my car or my father's truck and went to see Mrs. Daughter at the hospital. I recall the scene at what was then a very tiny Kentwood Hospital. It was the same small town hospital where I had somehow survived as a baby (with measles and pneumonia). Now, Mrs. Daughter was in one of the small rooms, fighting for her life. None of the younger children were permitted in to see her, so I gathered them, and we quietly made our way along the outside of the hospital until we came upon the windows of her room. When my mother saw us out there, she opened a window, and all the kids peered in at this great friend of our family—lying there, trying to smile back at us, still happy to take part in whatever our family was doing.

She had been a fighter, every day since she had learned of her diagnosis. Even when they told her she'd have to stop smoking, she didn't. She said she would die the way she lived. I believe she was puffing on a cigarette that night, with all of us there. She didn't have regrets standing in the way of her leaving this life. The way we stood outside that window though, I'll never forget it. Until then, I hadn't really thought about death or the fact that one day the people I loved the most would, one by one, leave this world.

The Guardian

> ... of a noble bearing always, good guardians of themselves and of the music which they have learned, and retaining under all circumstances a rhythmical and harmonious nature, such as will be most serviceable to the individual and to the state.
>
> —PLATO, THE REPUBLIC[1]

Did you ever knock at the front door of a person who is dying and stare into her eyes—cold, yet living, and glistening in idle search for release?

A hard reminder, you say to yourself, and you go on in.

And there on the wall is a picture of her loving husband, who has recently passed away. He looks sixty-ish, graying, distinguished like a minister or a school principal from way back. And you remember him back then, sitting in the pulpit after he got sick the first time, and you feel his roving eyes—pinpointed lasers from where you sit near the back of the church—wearing you down and making you behave like a civilized child should, like a good little black girl who has grown up in the South, and like any child who walked through those hallowed, sacred doors of your now

---

1. Plato, *The Republic*, 381 BC.

defunct school where he was principal. You remember all this now, as you follow her to just feet inside the door, to where she'll sit, in a rocker that has its back to the TV room. You'll take a seat in a very coiffed, almost immaculate sitting room, where only the few are admitted these days since she has become so ill. "She has to limit her visitors," the community of well-wishers often whispers. You feel lucky because you've known all along that you aren't all that special, but you are to her. And as she sits, softly, her 68-year-old body achingly fragile, yet glowingly distinct, her aesthetic beauty is still visible—a force that has always penetrated, protected, and empowered her.

Some things just last, you think to yourself.

You don't talk, as usual. With her, words jump out of your mouth like surprises at parties and like pranksters leaping out of bushes late at night. You remember the card that you're holding in your hands. It's the reason you've come.

You've just returned from Europe. Somehow, you manage to tell her all that you've done while flirting with life and time overseas: the tour of favorite castles, the Squares, the Palaces, the ethnic restaurants every night. How you almost missed Paris. How you later stood near the top of the Eiffel Tower at sunset and felt, for a moment, that you had reached the penultimate moment of your life. How you drove through so many countries that you cannot keep track of them now. Of the double-decker buses and the roundabouts, the never-ending vineyards, and the bathrooms without proper toilets. You go on and on, and she listens, intently, with a smile that never leaves. You see her heart is getting fuller.

That is when you give her the card. It is from St. Paul's church in London, you say.

And she reads it, not just to herself, but out loud, as though this will be the first time you hear it as well. And her voice is still distinct: wavy, grainy, sweet like it's imploring. And you think back to the first grade when your class is practicing for the school recital and you are sick and she tells you to lie down on the bench with your head on her lap. And you can still feel her stomach move in and out, in and out, like it is life's only signal, or proof that everything is real. And her voice carries, over you, over the bleachers, and over the gymnasium floor, to the students, your fellow classmates. And they listen to her because she is their teacher and because she is the most thoroughly perfect person they may ever know.

And you hear her reading the card from St. Paul's:

Jesus said, 'I am the light of the world. No follower of mine shall walk in darkness' (John 8:12). A candle is a reminder. It recalls Jesus, the one true light, whom the darkness could not extinguish. A candle is a parable; burning itself out, it gives light to others. A candle is a symbol. It speaks of light, hope, warmth and love. A candle is a sign. It reminds us of the prayers of God's people. Jesus said, 'Let your light shine.' (Matthew 5:16)

When she has read the final line, she seems relieved that she doesn't have to read anymore. But she can look. And she can see you, even through eyes bulging with tears.

And you say to her, "I lit a candle for you, there. And I prayed that you would be okay." You don't tell her that you knelt down on the red carpeted *prie-dieu* and closed your eyes, as if to the world forever, and clasped your hands in supplication, asking God to take care of her, in this world as well as the next, to always keep her safe, and close, no matter what. You don't say that you asked specifically that her life be spared, or at the least, that her pain be taken away.

You don't tell her that you asked all of this in the name of friendship, or that before you ended the prayer your mind went scatterbraining back to the day you became friends, when Maury and Nitara and Malik were walking with you into the church, back to your church's kitchen. The tables were filled with food for your mother's Annual Senior Citizens' Dinner. It was the holidays and everyone gathered festively. Most of the elderly were too old or too sick to come, but plates were prepared. One kind soul had promised to journey through the community, dropping off the food with the season's greetings. And there she came, once again in red, the color which most pleased her senses, though as a missionary, she more often wore white.

It's Christmas red, you had thought.

She saw you standing there, with your visiting friends, and came to greet you—her soft, failing hands and arms reaching out to meet you. As usual, a hug and a kiss. Introductions were begun, but before you could blurt out her name, she took control of the process and told these new friends that she was an old friend of yours. And your heart melted because until that moment you'd only thought of yourself as her student, as a fellow church member, as someone who lived in the same community, as co-humans on this great planet, but never as friends.

Sometimes a moment eclipses a day, or a lifetime, or eternity. In that moment, as you stood there surrounded by friends—people you'd never wish to trade—you became a little girl again and your family was poor and you looked up to people like her because teachers were the guardians of your little world: they were educated and were the uncontested leaders of your community; they believed in the proper values of right and wrong; they wore fine clothes and drove the best cars, they spoke nice and proper; and they wanted you to grow up to do and have the same things. They encouraged you always to do and be your best, and you wanted to because you respected no one more.

You remember that she had come to your house—after Greg Martin had run into you and you fell backwards and struck your head on a piece of jagged concrete. And you remember her rushing you, in her own car—with the blood running down your face and onto the vinyl seat—to the nearest doctor. You feel how soft and reassuring her hand felt against your own. She never once let go of you as your head was being stitched up. You took the candy sucker she gave you then, for being a good girl and not crying so much. Then you remember the warm flowery smell of her car as she drove you home, and how extraordinarily well you felt when she helped your mother put you to bed. And as they both walked through your bedroom door, you saw the reverence your mother gave this teacher, this woman who you, even with your broken head, could tell was special—not only because she was a teacher, but because of who she was as a person.

So, you sit there, in her home, opposite her, in a straight-back chair, listening to this former teacher who has become your friend in the final years, as she desperately tries to tell you how much this token of a card means to her. And you don't question God that day, or nature, or any of those things that seem so awfully important but in the end usually just blends into miniscule pieces of truth and knowledge. You realize that every truth you've ever needed to know is right there, in that one moment.

She tells you that she is crying because you thought of her, that even when you went half way around the world, you'd still think of her.

But time is short, this day.

She must save her strength. The cancer has spread, she says, and the chemo and the meds keep her so tired. She wants to live, to get outside that house.

"You'll have to take me for a ride in that sports car of yours," she says.

And of course, you agree, but somehow, it never happens.

Old Man Carves an Ax Handle

He is old, much like the last days of youth, or when a new beginning is inevitable.

His black hands are gnarled like the angles and curves of the Sunny Hills—the Louisiana hillsides where he was born and raised, and has spent most of his days, other than that stint in the war.

His fingers are long and thick at the edges, from the years having taken advantage; they have a bony hollowness about the knuckles—like emaciated animals having survived the worst of winter. They are ashy and tired and in need of relief.

He sits upon the woody oak stump in the morning sun of springtime, his overalls worn into the mold of his life's movements. The slender piece of wood, hickory in scent, rests upon his knee—it is straight wood, no knots, and not too aged.

He will trim the rougher spots, then wood file the length of the handle, dressing it down, making it slick to his touch. Tender strips of wood will lie, as if they've died there, in gentle piles upon the ground. Tiny white chips and flakes will cover his hands like woody gloves against the elements. There is order in his movements; nothing is unimportant.

When he has finished whittling, molding, and filing down, he will force the newly made handle into the ax. Then he will begin again.

He will carve two ax handles today, two tomorrow, and two the next day, every day for many weeks, and then sell them for $6.00 each. He also carves hoe handles, and handles for hammers and hatchet blades.

"They buy them as fast as I can make them," he says, proudly, confidently. "I don't mind, though, 'cause you gotta stay busy in life. You can't just sit around or you'll get left behind—and that's as sure as 1-2-3."

Willie Vern

Around the same time that my brother Lionel died, my oldest sister Willie developed a rash that first appeared on her face then mobilized itself over her arms and legs. My mother painstakingly made the rounds to hospitals and clinics, but none of the doctors knew what it was. The rash turned to lesions and irritated my sister so abominably that she would lie in bed and cry. Her soft screams could be heard from her bedroom late at night as the rest of the family tried, but was not able to sleep. At church, she would stand from where she was seated and ask the pastor and the entire congregation to pray for her. At home, she would scratch herself until she bled, unable to stop the undeniable itch that seemed to come from deep within. All of this I heard from my mother across the phone lines, for I lived in Wisconsin at that time, working as an over-the-road truck driver, and I rarely came home to Sunny Hill then.

I began moving back to Louisiana in the early nineties. At one of the few dinners where most of the family was together—my father, my mother, and most of the siblings—we sat around the dinner table talking about trivial things, that is, until my father stood up and uncharacteristically said, "I love y'all." He had recently been diagnosed with prostate cancer, and would lose two of his brothers to cancer. I remember this moment of my father's confession so well because he continued talking, even though our faces were stunned into silence at having heard him say those words.

He thanked the Lord for his family. He praised us for giving him so much support over the years. He was proud to have his family near at such a time. When he said all this, his eyes tactfully skipped over to me, like he wasn't sure I was actually there.

At that moment, I knew he thought I had come home for him. Although I loved him in my own way, I still hadn't forgiven him for all the years that he seemed to have forgotten how to love my mother, based on the way he had treated her over those years. And yet, in my heart, I, too, wasn't sure that I hadn't moved home because of his diagnosis.

But as we crowded around a dinner table that we had long ago outgrown, I sensed the bare presence of my oldest sister Willie, perched in her favorite chair in the living room, her feet placed on the top rung of the chair's structure. She sat there, nibbling at food that was piled high in an old cake pan she was using as a plate.

When I had walked through the front door that afternoon, and saw Willie sitting in that same chair, against the wall that connected the living room and the dining room, I had not known what to do. In the many months of conversations with my mother, she had said, "You won't recognize Willie." At that moment, when I saw her, I wanted to go back to any one of those conversations with my mother and press her for more information: how long has she been like this? When did it get this bad? What do the doctors say? Is it okay to touch her?

Perhaps sensing my apprehension, Willie simply said, "Hey, you finally made it, huh?" Yes, I had, but if I could have, I would have turned around and gone back to Wisconsin, or at the very least, I would have thrown myself beneath the musty brown carpet on the living room floor, and stayed there indefinitely. I was shocked by what I saw, at what my sister had become.

Sitting on the other side of the dining room wall was a practice she had taken up long before she became sick (perhaps because from that position, she could see the TV). But now, it seemed necessary that she station herself there, away from everyone else. I knew she was perched on her chair, with her knees up, hovering over a pan filled to the edges with food, picking at some morsel—probably cake, her favorite. But I intentionally did not think of her face and her arms and her legs, which were all covered in a dark pithy scalyness that made me want to puke. She seemed so far away from the person I had always known; it was like her real self had been dislocated, or lost completely, or perhaps eaten up by this hideous new body that I saw.

I don't remember when they decided Willie was "mentally retarded," but it must have been when I was very young. Perhaps I don't remember because I never believed it was so. To me, Willie was tenacious, energetic, and capable. As the oldest, she cared for the rest of us—Lionel, Venesta, David, and me, as well as all the subsequent siblings that would be born—when my mother would leave us in her charge. She had that same type of silence about her that is endemic to my entire family; only it was poignantly special in her. Life emanated from the core of her. She literally spent every minute of every day doing something. It was she who kept the leaves swept in the yard, and it was she who planted and tended the numerous flowerbeds around our house. My father always said of her, "That girl'll be workin' right up to the day she die. On her way to the casket, she'll bend down and pick up somethin' off the floor." He never made a truer statement.

Actually, I believe her character became tainted by association, having spent so much time with our cousin, Eddie Joe, who obviously had some problems. Eddie Joe became another of our sisters when her mother, Josephine—my mother's sister—died in an automobile accident. The year that both Willie and Eddie Joe were born, 1947, people still thought of bed-wetters, slobberers, and overtly happy people—all of which Eddie Joe was—as mentally retarded. It was probably some meddling do-gooder who had tagged Willie with the label as well.

My mother had felt pressured or forced by her community to take Willie out of elementary school as well. Willie and Eddie Joe were always so close, in their friendship and trust in one another that perhaps Willie preferred to embrace the misconception rather than rally against it. She didn't care about small things like what other people thought of her. But like any rumor, this false marker of who she was got substituted for the truth, and over the years it ate away at her original self.

There had been the summers so many years before when my mother had sent my sister Venesta and me with Willie to work picking vegetables on whoever's farm was hiring that week. Often, my brother Lionel would go as well.

On the way to the fields, the truck would stop at the neighborhood grocery store so that everyone could buy their lunch. We'd dismount and go tearing through the store searching for sardines, potted meat, crackers, a slice or two of bologna (more if he or she could afford it), Lays potato chips, and Fanta sodas. Willie would always get sardines and crackers and a grape soda. Venesta alternated between bologna and potted meat, and I would settle for a mayonnaise sandwich—I wasn't crazy about eating meat. Someone in the group would buy Sunbeam bread and a small jar of mayonnaise, and everyone would share in it. On the days that we bought the bread, I'd eat as many slices as I could before someone stopped me, and then drink my hot strawberry soda.

When we arrived at the field, we'd be given either a ten-gallon bucket or a large burlap sack that had a rope or a sturdy piece of cloth attached to the open end. We'd take up the bucket or sling the sack over our shoulders and go to the nearest row of beans, peas, peppers, or cucumbers and commence picking until lunchtime.

When strawberry picking season came, we were sent to work on one of the strawberry farms in Independence or Amite. Once, I went home having made only a pittance of the money that Venesta and Willie had made, and all because I ate most of the strawberries I put my little fingers on. Not only was I sick that night, but my mother was so upset she didn't send me back to the strawberry farm for the rest of that season.

I remember that there was always an abundance of some "thing" that needed to be picked. That particular summer, we also went to pick up Tung oils, which all of us hated. These dark, sticky, and habitually reeking balls usually covered the ground's surface beneath the unlimited rows of Tung oil trees. It soon became a family affair, and more often than not, we would back up to the nearest Tung oil tree, disembark from the truck, and commence to picking up every dark, sticky ball we could find.

Sometimes we would work for a man who planted turnip greens. The purple and white heads of these giant greens grew to the size of a grapefruit. When I told my mother about the greens, she laughed and said, "Those are what rich folk call rutabagas." I didn't care what they were called, I was merely happy to be in their presence. I marveled at their texture and color. I felt as though it was me against them. When I'd grab hold and try to pull them out, on the ground I'd land. Willie, who was by far the best worker in the parish, would pick two of her own rows then come down and meet Venesta and me on our rows before we got half way up the rows. She would go behind me pulling up all the heads that I had missed so that I wouldn't get yelled at by the boss man.

At lunch, I would be so tired that I could hardly move, but I'd look over at Willie, sitting with her food propped up on her knee, and nibbling on her sardines. She looked like she could work all day. Maybe she knew how much we needed the money. "Hurry up," she'd tell us, "the man'll be calling us back any minute." And sure enough, in just about a minute, the man would come, telling us to get back to work.

I remember a particular Sunday, when I was about twelve or so, I saw Willie as though I were seeing her for the first time. We were riding on the back of the family vehicle (a Chevy short-bed truck) and my father was driving, as my mother always said, like the devil was on his tail. The girls had to hold their dresses down with one hand and hold on to the side of the truck bed with the other hand. Our hair whipped across our faces and left stinging marks as witnesses.

Although my eyes were partly closed, I noticed Willie smiling at me. It was a gentle, almost helpless smile. Her skin had a glowing smoothness, in a rich brown caramel. She had gained some weight, and her print dress was tight across her bosom. But she didn't look fat; her skin wrapped around her in a satisfied pleasantness. It occurred to me that she was the most beautifully colored of all our family. I wondered if it was because she was our half-sister. None of us knew—including Willie—who her father was. That was the one thing my mother didn't talk about, and we knew better than to ask.

But then, in that moment, as I was looking at Willie, I noticed. She saw me looking at her and motioned for me to come sit next to her. She moved over on the bench that was positioned against the back of the cab of the truck. After that, we sat there like friends, enjoying the coolness of the breeze that blew just above our heads.

About six months before my brother Lionel died, we celebrated our parents' 50th Wedding Anniversary (Valentine's Day, 1998). Someone, probably my baby sister, suggested that all the children march down the aisle in a short program as part of the wedding. Most of the siblings agreed, but as the wedding program coordinator, it was up to me to make it happen. A short program before the wedding seemed harmless enough, until I thought of Willie, who was born before my parents were married. I thought of my mother and wondered whether or not she'd want her past life dredged up like some wet, smelly thing brought out in the sun's light. I knew I would have to speak to my mother face to face. At that point, I had moved to New Orleans proper, so I made the hour and a half drive to Sunny Hill on a weekday morning, at a time when I thought she could talk.

I remember vividly my mother sitting on the sofa watching *The Young and the Restless* when I arrived. After our perfunctory greeting, a kiss on opposite right cheeks, I sat next to her, but it was almost an hour before I could pose the question that I had come to ask.

"Momma," I said, in a voice lower than usual. "You know I'm putting together the program for the wedding, right?"

She nodded, "Unh, hunh."

"We're thinking about having all the children, from the oldest to the youngest, march in as the wedding narrator tells the audience a little about each child. That way, we could revisit the past fifty years through the births of your children." I waited for something from my mother, but she seemed more interested in what Nick and Sharon were doing on TV than her second wedding. Finally, I said, "Momma, what do you think?"

Slowly her head turned to the left and then tilted up in that way we knew meant she was presently sad or disgusted with life. I followed her eyes. They were stuck on Willie, who sat in her chair against the wall—her right arm on her knees and her left hand moving up and down her scarred, blackened legs. Her eyes and that one arm that moved seemed to be the only living things on her.

I said, "We don't have to do this, Momma. That's why I came to ask you about it."

My mother returned her attention to the soap opera on television. When a commercial came on, she smiled and said that she didn't care; that maybe I should ask my father since the wedding meant so much to him.

My father thought it was a great idea. Since my father's cancer diagnosis, he had done everything in his power to prove his love for my mother, including insisting on this grand celebration of their fifty years together. To him, all of it would make for a perfect day. And perhaps he thought it would make up for all the pain he'd caused over the years. But on the day of the wedding, as we all lined up to march in, and I saw Willie standing at the front of the line, the first of the ten children that would march in, suddenly I felt nauseated just thinking of how bad of an idea this really was.

As Willie began to march up the aisle of the church, Louise, our cousin and the narrator of the wedding program, in an effort not to embarrass my mother, began by jokingly referring to how my parents had first met (two of my father's brothers had already married two of my mother's sisters, so my father had run all the way to my mother's parents' house hoping to get the last sister who was not married—this was my mother). As Willie moved down the aisle, her frail body tilted from side to side like it was one big muscle. Her burgundy velvet dress hid everything but her damaged face, neck, and hands. A white laced chapel cap covered a head that was almost bald, with the exception of a few delicate patches of hair.

Louise rambled on about insignificant things. But it was the things that she left out that I started to remember. With each step that Willie took, I went further back, as though I had actually been there when she was born—a year before my father married my mother. I imagined my father's smug twenty-nine-year-old face, thinking he was doing my fourteen-year-old mother a favor by marrying her. I imagined my mother's father—the head deacon at church—disgraced and grateful that any man would confess love for his daughter and mean it enough to marry her. Then my eyes began to open, and I saw my life as a toddler and young girl; my father coming home at the pitchest hours of darkness; my mother telling me to go back to sleep—me, awakened by yet another dream of falling or being chased by vicious animals. I saw the fights between them that sometimes stumbled over into the next day. I saw Willie hit my father with the iron cover of a milk can until he stopped strangling my mother. Then I began to hear as well. I heard my mother talking to us, saying, "Never hate him, he's your father." As the years passed, I heard her say, "You don't need nobody who can't give you something you can get for yourself." And I heard her say, "Don't let your life be full of regrets."

When I looked up, Willie had made it half way down the aisle. Everyone stared at her, the same way I had stared when I first came home from my travels and saw the conspicuous disease that had taken over her body. As Willie marched up the aisle, I started to feel bitter knowing that there was no chance for her to walk down that aisle as a bride, and because of the diseased condition of her skin, she would never wear white again.

There had probably been lots of guys over the years. I used to hear her singing Wilson Picket's "I'm in Love." I knew there was one guy for certain; his name was Rayford. Willie had a crush on him when she was in her twenties. Every time she saw him she'd light up like a firefly stuck on bright. She confided in my very young self: "I sure do like me some Rayford." After that, I would tease her unmercifully: "Willie likes Rayford. Willie's gonna marry him!" She would giggle a child's laugh, until I'd threaten to tell our mother. Then she'd chase me around the house and across the open field in back of our house. She was a child wasting away in a woman's body.

Yet, there she was, on the day of my parent's 50th wedding anniversary, almost fifty-one years old, her body disfigured by an unrelenting disease—and she was smiling. As she sat down on the bench, waiting for the rest of us to march in, she had that same grin that I'd seen on the truck years before when she shared her seat with me. Something burst inside of me. I wouldn't have been surprised to see a tear run down her face, but the inviolate joy that was looking back at me was too much. When my turn came to march in, I was wiping away my own tears.

On the night of September 13, 2000, I was at my apartment in New Orleans, sipping on a glass of wine when the phone rang. It was a family friend who lived in Sunny Hill, who called to inform me that Willie had been taken to the hospital. She said Lacey (my niece) and I, who were the only two immediate family members who were not in Sunny Hill, needed to get to the hospital as quickly as we could.

When I finally walked into the ICU waiting room and saw my mother slumped down into a chair, unable to get up and greet me with her usual kiss on the cheek, all of it became a revelation to me. Our eyes met, and she burst into tears. Then I burst into tears—so many tears that in many ways, they still have not stopped.

Around dinnertime the next day, most of Willie's family and friends crowded around my mother, who sat in the same chair, not having moved since she'd arrived the evening before. She was stuck there, surrounded by a grief that seemed to engulf her like water flooding into a room. We all knew what she was thinking: within two years she had lost her firstborn son and now . . . well, we didn't know.

Everyone who came brought food. The waiting room at this small town hospital became so full that other families with loved ones in intensive care were forced to join in with our family, or re-station themselves in the chapel. And there I was, the oldest of my mother's children present, feeling desolately alone, and making decisions I didn't want to make: who would be allowed to see Willie and when; acting as referee between battling friends, all vying for a position at the top of our family's list of confidants "at a time like this"; and eventually, when we would turn off the life support system for Willie.

I greeted aunts, uncles, and cousins, and repeated the latest news over and over. I thought of my sister Venesta, who would now become the oldest proper, but she sat at Gatwick Airport in London trying to get a flight out. Because we were so close in age (a year apart), she and I had been brought up like twins. My mother often dressed us in the same outfits. People rarely saw one of us without the other. She was the tall one; I was the short one. She was the talker; I was the thinker. She searched for people to fight; I searched for people to love. And now, she was the one missing; and I was the one present. I cursed her absence under my breath.

At some point in the afternoon, the doctor came in and told us that there was no hope, that Willie had gone into cardiac arrest and though they revived her, it was only a matter of time. For all intents and purposes, she was gone. He would also later tell us that all of Willie's organs were eaten up so badly that he had no idea how she had survived as long as she did. Her liver and kidneys had all but stopped functioning. Her heart was the size of a basketball. He said that because the kidneys weren't working properly, toxic waste had only found a release through her skin, a final explanation for the demolishment of her skin over the final years of her life. We were told that Willie probably had a rare form of Lupus that silently attacks the organs and mimics so many other diseases that it's hard to diagnose; and because it wasn't diagnosed within the early stages of development, it was later impossible to control. On that day, after the news of her final prognosis was delivered, the doctor left the room and allowed us to make the decision as to when we would "let her go."

Most people don't believe this, but about a month before Willie died, I dreamed that a train was bearing down on my parents' house. I ran from room to room warning everyone to get out before the train tore through the house. When the train arrived, it pulled up alongside the house, just beyond one of the two hundred-year-old oak trees in the front yard, and stopped. I stepped on the train. I noticed that there were no empty seats onboard. Most of the people sat looking straight ahead, their faces gray and motionless. I looked to the rear of the train and saw what appeared to be my sister (though it wasn't a particular sister, but a composite of all of them) and two children, the younger of which looked remarkably like me as a child. Clothed in bright colors, these three people clashed against the grayness of everyone else on the train.

Suddenly, the train started to move again, and I told my sister that we must get off. "Hurry!" I yelled at her, "Get the kids, we've got to jump!" One of the two children, the smallest one who looked like me, ran to the front of the train where I stood and took my hand. I wrapped her in my arms and jumped. When I looked back at the train, which had picked up speed and was already far beyond me, I saw my sister standing at the ledge where I had stood. She was holding the hand of the other child. Soon, the two of them disappeared from my sight, leaving only the chugging, helpless sounds of the death train.

The day after the doctor spoke to us about Willie's condition, as many of us as could fit into her small room stood looking down on her for the last time. All of the tubes had been disconnected and she lay there like an exhibit at the fair. I couldn't help but notice the grayness of her face; it was swollen and all the color had drained from it. As the last essence of her life circled the room then drifted into its next realm, I thought of that dream; only it didn't seem like a dream anymore. It was the real and careless way I had treated my sister since she'd fallen ill. I saw myself jump off the death train and leave her behind. In the court of decency, I would be found guilty of having none. In this moment, I felt as though I was unbuttoning the cleavage of my soul. I saw that I had never helped Willie the way she had helped me. If I couldn't make some of her dreams come true, I could have at least asked her about them. No, I was too damned busy removing myself from the bad situation that was often our family's life. I had figuratively jumped off the train and left her, but I had literally left her over the years to fend for herself in a world that didn't seem to care so much about her. Somehow, she had seemed content to just belong, to be a member of our imperfect family; to love a father who wasn't hers and who often mistreated her; to have a mother who loved her as best she could because she was a child herself when she brought Willie into the world.

Mostly, I thought about how much she had cared for me, and now she was gone. It's funny how regrets keep us from letting go. One of the hardest things I had to do in my life was learn to say goodbye to Willie Vern.

The River

I can only recall one day that I spent alone with my parents. I was thirty-four years old. My father had recently been diagnosed with prostate cancer, and although all the doctors said that if he had to get cancer this was the best kind to get, we were all still worried about his survival rate. But through all the diagnoses and going back and forth to the VA hospital, something had changed within my father: he almost instantly became the husband my mother always knew (or at least suspected) he could be. He was suddenly devoted to her, spent his waking hours waiting on her hand and foot, rarely leaving her side for the next ten or so years. And even though he was much older, it would be she who would die first and free him from his marital vows. Vows, of course, that until he was diagnosed with cancer, he had quite often not paid attention to.

So my parents and I went fishing off the Mississippi River near Laplace, Louisiana. But that day didn't have to be a rarity for me to remember it so vividly. I remember because it may have been the most perfect day of all my days here on earth. I was on a break from college and had been spending quiet, irresistible weeks with my family in Sunny Hill. Those were the elaborate times when my father's cancer had first gone into remission; before my mother had fallen into diabetes and an arthritic hip; and before I'd gotten so busy in life that I had to be ill myself before I would think of slowing down.

My mother and father were ardent fishers, always had been. When we were children and there was no work to be done, my father sought out fishing holes no matter how small or irreverent. Sometimes we stood on the banks of some kind stranger's pond, dodging snakes that slithered through the soggy, tall grasses and snapping turtles that invariably ended up on the ends of our fishing poles, having eaten all the bait and were then too obstinate to let go. Sometimes the turtles were so big that the pole would break, leaving us searching through the summer's heated woods or on the sides of roadways to find another length of bamboo to take its place.

Creeks and narrow riverbeds became our favored places to fish, where we found our greatest success—the luck always jumped us like a drowning man into a boat. Over the years, we had edged our way up the sculptured sides of rivers like the Bogue Chitto, the Pearl, and the Tangipahoa. We had hitchhiked deep into woods shadowed with the thickness of crowded trees, following curling creeks as their banks came and receded and came back again.

There was always some "spot" to be had, and only my father knew exactly where it was. Once he found it, everyone relinquished their gear—usually my parents, brothers and sisters and me, but also their friends, our friends, or anyone who was fortunate enough to be invited on the fishing party. My father never went fishing alone. I'm not sure if it was because black people didn't go traipsing through just anybody's woods without backup, or simply because most people didn't go fishing alone. Black bears were rare, but rumor set their reputation as pretty fierce. And I'm sure there were other dangers lurking in those pristine barely touched woods. I choose to think that my father could have gone fishing by and for himself if he'd wanted to, but being that he loved our company so, simply chose not to.

I believe that most fishing trips are successful by nature—the fisher person finds joy in peaceful solitude with nature's surroundings. When my mother and father and I left that warm April morning, we had already found that peace in our minds: our day would be spent sitting on buckets, waiting for that elusive bite, swatting flies and mosquitoes, pulling in maybe one or two catfish, yet never doubting that the next, biggest catch was on the horizon. The many fishing trips we'd taken along the river had left us almost oblivious to the river's sweet melancholic beauty, so that as we drove along River Road on the eastern edge of Laplace, our only concern was to find the spot where the fish were abundant and hungry.

My father's truck at that time was an old sky blue Chevy that had once gotten stuck on the Chalmette ferry because the key broke off in the ignition. Actually, my father and mother and one of their friends had ridden back and forth on the ferry until my sister showed up with an alternate key. The truck looked older than its age, and chugged more than purred or rumbled. Because my mother always sat in the middle, next to my father, no matter how many people were crammed onto the truck's seat, her girth caused my father to take up the habit of shifting gears with his right hand through the steering wheel. This obviously wasn't a task he had mastered because more often than not, he'd simply forego the shifting, and when he came to a stop light or some other object that impeded his progress, he would leave the truck in its traveling gear rather than shift back down until he found the first, starting gear again.

As we searched for a place to lay our poles and cast our reels, my father's truck blew heavy breaths, sounding as though it was relentlessly suffering and would stop breathing at any moment. My mother, forever one to comment on the obvious, said to my father, "Shift, Oscar, shift." But before my father could do so, he turned sharply onto a white graveled path that led up to the top of the levee.

"This is it," my father said. Apparently, we'd been there before. My mother and I looked at each other, which meant that we doubted it. My father was sure of it. Just beyond the levee, the gravel path turned into a slightly worn path that parted the overgrown brush. My father, never fearful, proceeded to follow the makeshift road, ever sure that the river would meet us at the end. And sure enough, it did. After a few hundred yards, the still greening trees began to thin out, and we could see the river briskly running before us.

Sometimes the anticipation of pleasure overstimulates us, and when we, at last, reach the moment that our desire is realized, the climactic moment pales in comparison. But that short minute it took to get beyond the edge of the trees could never compare to the way the mighty Mississippi looked to me when we finally reached it. Suddenly my life seemed all glossy and beautifully snapped. The sun seemed to shine that day only for the purpose of bathing the river in its radiance. Tiny sparkles of light glistened off the water as the river turned and bubbled and expanded and contracted in its giant flow. The blue from the sky was exact when it touched the mirrored river. There were no errant limbs or discarded trash floating downstream, and no large cumbersome tanker grinding through the water, dredging up the river's sleeping mud. All this I could see from where I sat, in my father's truck, next to my mother, who also sat disbelieving the postcard vista before us.

When we finally gathered our courage to venture out and prove that this was no mirage, we saw beneath us a spotless, beige sandy beach. Years before, while in the U. S. Navy, I had been stationed in Hawaii, and had often taken a short flight from Honolulu to Maui for the weekend. There on Maui, I had seen some beaches—beaches I thought were the most flawless in all the world—yet, here before me, lay the comparable: a gorgeous sunny beach off the normally dark and musky Mississippi. My father and mother and I walked up to the very edge of the river, crunching through the sand as it ate at our feet, then set down our buckets, poles, hooks, and rods.

I almost cry when I think of the illimitableness of our peace that day. After my father hooked our rods, he intended to distance himself from us, like he always did, by a hundred yards or more, but my mother, who rarely moved after she found her spot, who sat down on her bucket as if she needed to state the movement's finality, called my father back, informing him that he had not cast her rod before he left. After all our rods were thrown, and we could barely see our lines against the brightness of the water's glow, we sat quiet for the first time. My father hated noise when he fished—he never discounted the intelligence of non-humans; he always said that fish would hear us and would know not to jump onto our hooks. So, we sat still and quiet, mesmerized by our fishing lines dancing with the water.

As I sat there, I thought back to the second grade, to a time when I wasn't quite sure of where I belonged. I had walked up to my teacher—actually, I had asked my best friend Lorraine to do it—and told my teacher that I was coming home with her. I had every intention of going to live with this teacher forever. My mother and father, though undoubtedly embarrassed that one of their many children would want to leave them, did not try to stop me. My mother packed a bag for me, placing inside it my favorite red pajamas, a clean dress for the next day's school, and my best underwear.

As I sat there on my fishing bucket that day, waiting for unintelligent fish to jump onto my hook, I suddenly felt aware of how my parents must have felt when they sent me off to school that morning long before. It was the first time that I had been away from them, and the only time, perhaps, that they may have felt like failures as parents.

I glanced down the beach to where my father sat in a curve in the river. He was off his bucket, pulling in his line to check it for bait. He looked like a fisherman, truly. At 5' 11" and 160 pounds my father has always been thin; his dirty blue overalls hung over his shoulders like a blanket thrown across a clothes line—there was no shape to be seen, with the exception of his chest, which poked upward and parallel to his chin. The cotton buttoned shirt underneath his 'ralls was rolled up past his unusually dark brown elbows. Although he was 74 years old then, his face was covered only by a few days growth of beard and a few wrinkles that sliced across his forehead. He wore a baseball cap that he'd gotten from some finance company in either Kentwood or Franklinton. Every few minutes or so, he would glance in my mother's direction, and seeing that she was still sitting with the pole leaning against her right leg, staring off beyond our presence, he would turn back to his reeling.

About three years before our perfect fishing trip, my father had decided he would devote his life to helping others. At the core of my father was now a good man who understood his mortality and who feared God—he was truly sorry for any harm that he had caused others, especially those within our family. At the very top of that list was my mother. And God. He stood up at one Sunday church service and declared that he had been called to preach the gospel. After that, wherever he went he told those who would listen that he had once been a great fisherman, that he had caught many fish during his lifetime, but that now, he had become a fisher of men, and he would try to pull in as many lost souls as he could before God called him home. That day in church, everyone had collectively remained silent at this news, but my mother, who sat in the Amen corner, had belted out a loud and triumphant "Amen" in support of her husband of over forty years. From that moment on, my mother and father had implicitly supported each other, heart and soul. She accompanied him to every church, storefront, or home he went to when and if he had a message that needed to be told. And he in turn attended to her, ever watchful of her every need, no matter how small. After all those years, they had finally become the perfectly tuned couple.

As soon as my father recast his rod, my mother turned to him, and he knew to come and pull in her line. I smiled thinking about it. My father pushed the grip end of his rod into the sand, and then came quickly to my mother. After he had dropped her line again, he made his way back to his own spot, and settled down once more.

I cannot say how long we waited for the first bite, for that first catfish to wade through the muddy bottom of the river and find and then devour

our struggling bait, but when the first fish struck, his piercing cry must have rung falsely throughout Fish Land. Soon our lines tugged hard and long against our rods, a sure sign that ol' brother catfish, as my father called the greatest of the fish, had eaten our bait.

We fished the better part of the late morning and into the early afternoon, never realizing that we hadn't eaten the sandwiches and chips and cold drinks that we had brought for lunch. By then, my father's fish bucket was filled with mostly medium sized catfish and red snappers. My father later caught a very large catfish that was so big (how big was it?) that it barely fit into the large ice chest that had held our drinks and sandwiches.

Around five o'clock that afternoon, we packed up our gear and headed back to Sunny Hill. On the way home, we laughed and talked about our good fortune. My mother and I still couldn't believe my father was bringing 'ol brother catfish home with us.

"Oh, he's too fat," my father complained.

"No, he'll eat good," my mother decided.

And I agreed.

Momma

You used to say,
    "You can walk with the devil,
    and he don't have to know
    you don't like him."
Like some Buddhist monk,
You managed to treat everyone the same:
With compassion,
Without preference—
With respect,
Like they were jewels
And you a common stone.

I admired you because
You'd insert yourself where others
Did not think you should be.
You had the daring assertiveness
Of a last child,
The belief that you
Deserved everything.

You sat all chummy
In the Ministers' Wives' Club;
Most of them educated,
Handsomely dressed,
Speaking proper—
You, never having eclipsed grade school,
In common, reduced-priced,
Often "Dollar Store" merchandise,
And with common sense speech.

You'd break into their conversations
Like the only way to gain access
Was to steal it,
And after a while,
You'd fit in;
You'd belong
Even more than they.

You knew everyone.
You knew how Big Baby and
Little Baby, the sisters,
Came about their nicknames, or
When was the first time Cousin Annie
Came to visit from Sneeds, Florida.
You even knew all of Daddy's people
On the Weary side of the Jameses.
You still knew the name of the woman
Who had put a hainch on your mother

MOMMA

Over forty years earlier.

You could name people off the street:
    "Yeah, that's so and so's cousin Edward.
    his daddy used 'ta pick cotton
    with my mother way back then."

The older you got, the less
Your tongue could hold its place.
At Sunday School, you
"Blessed out" the deacons
and everyone else, really,
For not doing their jobs.
    "My daughter," you said,
    "Sat down there in that hospital,
    sick as a dog, afraid of death
    knockin' on the door,
    that disease eatin' up her skin
    like acid been pour'd on it, and
    none of a y'all come
    ta' see about her."

And when that daughter, Willie,
Finally gave in,
Her body then gray from
Lifelessness,
The disease having eaten up
Her insides like it had the outer,
You sat in Riverside's waiting room,

Rocking back and forth—
With your large, swollen fingers clasped
Around a belly that sat comfortably
Upon your lap,
Your wet eyes
Closed to the world,
Your hair sticking up in little
Tuffs of pepper gray because
You didn't care then, or ever,
How you looked—
Your thinning lips mumbling
Your own prayer
As if you were speaking
Only to her, the departing,
Your first born, the child
You brought into this world
When you were
Yet a child yourself.
The one you carried every day
Thereafter,
Like a scarlet letter
Upon your breast.
You held on to her, your
Embarrassment for having sinned
Against God,
Family,
Community.

We all sat around you then, even

MOMMA

Some deacons,
And other church folk
Who had learned to come more often
And to care more for dying folk.
But you,
Didn't even know we were there.

And just beyond a year later,
You go that same route:
The slow ambulance—because
You lived so far and so deep
In the country,
In some small rural town,
A place people seldom know
"Where that is"—
The same heart, really,
Stopping,
Unable to fight,
Blocked from life, by
An embolism;
The restless years
Having worn it to pieces—
Pieces that no longer fit
The person
You had so painstakingly become.

And we rush to see you—
Those of us who live
"In the city"—

Though I am still sick
And can't rush anywhere these days,
But I sit in the passenger seat
Of Venesta's truck,
Headed to Riverside, again,
And I know you won't be there
When I get there.
And I try to remember when
Was the last time your body
Was warm.

Not even an hour before.
I talked to you on the phone,
Like I always talked to you.
You were worried, as usual,
About one of your children,
That life wasn't feeding her;
That people were mistreating her;
That the world wasn't big enough
To give her half the love you
Had spared up in your heart.
Your voice, you were lamenting, still
The death of three children
Already passed on.

When we arrive, at Riverside,
The place some people dare call "Killerside,"
We can't lay our heads on
Your warm soft skin,

MOMMA

Against your thigh, like
When we were kids,
Or gently on your arm, like
When we'd fallen asleep
Next to you in church,
Or on your shoulder, like
When we cried, and
Gave our troubles to you.

No.
You're cold already,
And beginning to stiffen,
And your color—
Though not gray, like
Willie's had been—
Is beginning to fade,
No longer important,
No longer a marker
For discerning folk
To decipher
Who you
Were supposed to be.

A year and a half later,
And I'm finally able to
Pick up your Bible from
My shelf—the shelf where
I've placed it,
And watched it,

Every day—
Like it would grow,
Or change,
Or become the thing
I want most—
A talking, living you.

David and I had talked—
Not my brother, but Nusloch—
And his memento is an old shirt
Of his father's.
    "If I could ever wear that shirt,"
    he says, "I know I could let him go."
And I understand the moment
Those words leave him
And find me.
I understand.

I pick up the Bible and
Open pages
Still covered
With the breath of you.
Your handwriting almost
Dances before me—so elemental,
So truly free, liberated
From pretentiousness.
You have notes from sermons,
And bookmarks—so many that you could
Go into business for yourself—

And programs, from church services
You attended when you
And Daddy
Traveled the highways,
Making yourselves home
At every church that
Opened its doors unto you.

And it's me crying now,
Rocking back and forth,
My large, full fingers
Wrapped around your Bible,
My eyes closed to the world,
My lips forming
My own prayer, and
Then the inevitable words,
    "You're gone.
    "You're gone."

And I wonder why it took so long
To start thinking of you that way,
Why I sometimes woke up thinking
Of your early morning calls,
Why so many of my dreams
Were of you and me
On a motorcycle,
On the open highway;
Why I could not cook
Your chicken pie until

Just the other day;
Why I still can't say goodbye,
For good, though I know
You want me to.

And then I remember
That you used to say,
    "Keep living."
And those words
Have a whole, new
Hopeful
Meaning.

Counting Children

My father, an uneducated though otherwise intelligent man, for years carried on a rather obvious and industrious love affair with a woman named Tabor who at first lived next door to us when I was yet a toddler and my brother, David, was still growing inside my mother's womb. At that time, our family ran a dairy for an older white couple who we children thought were our grandparents. My father came and went—much like the Guernsey and Holstein cows that came into the barn on early mornings, heavily laden with milk in their bags, dragging their rear hooves from the strain of it all. And like those cows, he then went out again, finding sustenance and comfort in fertile, desirable pastures when that day's milking was done. The Tabor woman's house sat directly across from the small gravel lane that led to the dairy. As my father made his way home on those evenings, although tired, he inevitably found strength in crossing the highway and directing himself to her door, as if he could not or would not walk the small distance farther to our house.

I know this because my mother often told us, her four children at the time, and subsequently over the years, the rest of us. Eventually the Tabor woman would move away, to a place where my mother's eyes could no longer see her so clearly—where the Tabor woman could no longer stand at the end of our driveway, unashamedly looking for even one sign of where our father might be. Back then, when my father was late returning home, or had gone into town, presumably to buy feed or other supplies for the dairy, my mother would say "He's probably with that woman."

Sometimes she'd pile us into the car, and go up and down the highways, ranting and driving, ranting and driving, as her gentle face turned into an edgy, mess of anger—all the while as our eyes petitioned her to stop. We were my mother's unwilling confidants then. My brother, Lionel, sitting in the front seat of the Pontiac, would say to her, "What we driving up and down the road for, Mama?" or "Mama, how long we gone drive around?" And my mother would answer without answering, her wetting eyes forcing my brother into silence. That look always said, "You got as much at stake as me, so sit there and be quiet."

I didn't hate my mother for forcing us to go on these wild tantrum trips or for blabbering on and on about my father. I was still lost in childhood whimsy. Besides, just as soon, my mother would flip the switch and we'd feel her special and generous kind of love, which seemed more apparent and real to me. We often resembled baby chicks, waiting for my mother to dole out a portion of whatever she had to us. No matter how many of us there were, she tried to treat us the same. We all tasted the piece of chocolate cake she had, or the one honey bun my father had brought her from the store, or the cola that was only a sip after it went around to each of us, but still tasted like the best thing we'd ever placed upon our waiting tongues. I marvel now, but she shared utterly everything with us—everything.

Despite my father's affairs, our family's life stream became a teeming, growing business. Our cousin Eddie became a sister after her mother died in a car crash. After David came Sampson, the fourteen-pounder that almost broke my mother's loins in two. Laura came in that dreaded year of '66. That year my father almost died when a tractor rolled and trapped him beneath its mammoth wheels, and my brother David's head was nearly crushed when he slipped and fell into the unyielding, steely belts of the fertilizer. When Hattie came in '69, my mother's closest friend, Mrs. Daughter, tried to grapple the baby from my mother's loving arms. It seems women were constantly asking my mother for her children. Over the years, we siblings grew proud and stood taller when we heard our mother say, once more, "No, I love all my children; I'm not giving any of them away." And the baby of the family came last; her birth brought on my mother's first heart attack and a condition that rendered her incapable of birthing any more children. No one said this was a blessing, but I'm sure we all thought it.

And when we had grown to be adults, fate or time or whatever deems it so, began to chip away our number. A vehicle struck down my oldest brother, Lionel, on a late July night as he walked home from a party. My oldest sister, Willie, who was then cursed and bathed in a rare disease, conceded her right to life when her heart, the size of a basketball, grew tired of supporting her and gave in, as her lungs and kidneys had already done, and as her worn, crusting and blackening skin and spirit had in those last days. Then we thought there would be another of us to go then because there, in the bucolia of a small town, superstition insisted that "death comes in threes." Which child would be that third? We all thought it. No one dared utter it.

My mother and father, though not always close, usually presented to the world a united and loving front. Although my father apparently had no qualms about showing his wife affection in public, he rarely did so. At their 50th wedding anniversary ceremony, after the minister had once again pronounced them husband and wife, my father had reached for my mother—her whole, large and graceful frame, pulled her close to him, and then kissed her with as much strength and passion as I had ever seen in movies or on television soap operas. My mother grabbed her veil, which already sat at the back of her head like it would fall helplessly to the floor, and allowed herself to be handled in that way by my father. Everyone who attended the wedding that day gasped—the church itself seemed to have done so—surprised by my father's blatant expression of passion for my mother. At home we children had rarely seen either show affection like this towards the other. But we accepted the kiss, like we accepted most things our father did, wrong or right.

Over the years, the neighboring children, our friends, and even people we met during the travelling years of our lives, had come to our house and witnessed the aura of my parents—the fact that they were still together, still devoted, and still trusting in their enjoined future. The picture they saw of my mother was brushed perfect. She grew into one of the best cooks in the area, often serving up dishpansful of her specialty, chicken pie. My mother lived out her numbered days concentrating on the welfare of others, with her children as her special charges. She genuinely wanted her children there with her. Sometimes she'd try to trick us into coming home, even though we had just visited with her a week before or even days before. She would call and say she had cooked our favorite meals, that we'd "better come and eat it." Sometimes she'd say in a bragging, boastful tone that one of us would be home, which might make the others jealous and come home as well. She made this same phone call to all her children. There was something so undeniable and liberating in knowing that we were at the center of her life.

And my father, too, developed a reputation among fathers. His barbecues often drew my friends out to the small, country town. He'd tell his wild, fantastic stories, and then hijack all newcomers to the back of the house. There, they'd see but not believe my father carry on conversations with the often wild and strange animals he captured and kept in pens. There was the rooster with the varied coat of red, green, white, and black. My father would sometimes carry the rooster on his shoulder and bring it into the house with him, even to my mother's protestations. At various times, he'd have possums, raccoons, and even wild rabbits locked up, but apparently enjoying every minute of their capture. Once there was a hawk that my brother had shot in the wing. My father nursed it back to health, feeding it milk and white bread. The animals seemed endless, much like the people who came over the years.

The visiting children, even when they had grown to be adults, always came back and grew accustomed to calling my parents "mother" and "father." My father often boasted, "Yeah, I got plenty chullin, all over the place. Sometimes people just walk up to me and say, 'Will you be my Daddy?'" But, we, his original children, who had grown accustomed to his riotous tales, would simply laugh or throw a cautious smile at him, as though he were crazy or wielding a weapon. We never expected the truth of it to just show up on our doorstep one day. And yet it did.

When the truth did come, it came like an unwelcome guest. It came like late and barren cows coming in from the pasture. And it came like old inevitable truth always comes, at the most inauspicious time.

After my mother passed away in December of 2001, three people claiming to be my father's children—by the Tabor woman—came to our house. They came from Mississippi, and they introduced themselves as our brother and sisters. Only a few weeks had passed. My mother's body had not time to settle into her underground home, and our tears of loss still burned on our disconsolate faces. But that day is clear. They came in a late model champagne-colored Camry, full of mysterious yet familiar looking people. As we looked out the front window of the old house, someone said, "That's Daddy's kids." I thought of Alice Walker's Africans in *The Color Purple* returning home to Celie after so many years. To those of us who had never known, for certain, that "Daddy's kids" existed, our eyes searched harder, with assiduous attention, trying to find reason and truth in the very shapes and semblance of their faces.

They came into the house and sat around, like we sat around, on sofas and the edges of sofas, on straight chairs that had been brought from the kitchen, and even on the end of my cousin Eddie's sick bed, which then inhabited the living room. And before our eyes, our family began to grow once more. There was the oldest son, who resembled my Uncle Jake as much as he did my father—he had my uncle's tall darkness and strong, proud face. His twin stood looking at our family's pictures on the walls; she actually favored me and my cousin Ruthie when we smile. Their sister came last. She sat next to me and insisted she and I shared my father's hands. It was then that my eyes turned on her, viciously, like my heart was beginning to turn on her because I knew even without looking that she and I did not share my father's thin, bony hands. There aren't many of my mother's genealogical traits and features that I possess, but one of them is her large, broad hands. Before I could stop myself from expressing my disdain, before I could hold my tongue, I said, sharply, to this new sibling, "No, these are my mother's hands." The next generation of nephews sat quietly and became even more hushed when I said these words to this new sister.

Everyone in the room sat quietly for a moment, taking in the obvious fact that we knew very little about each other. I wondered about the timeliness of the visit. Why would these half-siblings show up now, just after my mother had passed? I thought, passively, that the visit actually meant that had my mother still lived, none of them would be there. But, as we Jameses are apt to do, we sat silently, speaking only when questions were leveled at us, and we reserved our comments until our guests had gone. My sister Hattie, who lived in the family home with my parents, informed the rest of us that these siblings had actually come before; that my mother had met them; and that it was her wish that we all one day come to know each other. Hattie also informed us that my mother had actually attended the funeral of the Tabor woman some years earlier with our father. Then we were stunned and confused further, yet relieved that these strangers would not disrespect my mother by coming so soon after her death. And like we Jameses are also apt to do, we accepted the visit, just as we accepted the fact that the number of children had grown once more.

That was our beginning. A few months later, we all went to visit our new siblings. We went in the name of a barbecue, but lingered afterwards, taking pictures and talking and smiling at each other like we'd cared for one another all our lives. My father walked with a light and brisk step. He looked like he had stolen something valuable and was about to show it to the public. His new son-in-law had bought him a new pinstripe suit. None of us said it was too big or that it was way too youthful for his frame; we just allowed him to strut to his happy little beat.

    That night when I prayed, I talked to my mother at length. I knew she would approve, but I still felt for her. All those early years of my father's infidelities had come back. After I got off my knees and climbed into bed, I decided that I would not hold on to my mother's pain. Instinctively, I knew that while she lived she had let it go, and that I should do the same.

Daddy, It's Your Child Song

I see you standin' still
In waves across that hill.

Mickey didn't leave a light burnin'
Son gave striped marbles to Jake
Two more little black children
Catch a slow ride to Porter's store.

Laugh them green apples on the ground
Mother's tears come back around.

Bob, got cotton in that top field
Send Ethel, Dutch, Buddy Boy, and Marie
He the devil, spirit and all
Why everybody tryin' to beat it down?

My soul just standing still
As they all come back across that hill.

Bernice just up and married
Harriet goin' soon
Wipe the gin from your brow Papa
Hitch the mule; this day is long.

Mother wants them apples off the ground
Why all these years come back around?

I've never stopped trying to understand my father and the relationship he had with my mother. I know that, for instance, when he first returned from the Army as a young man, he came home to a woman—his first wife—who no longer loved him. This was news that greatly distressed him because for all the time that he had served his country, that he had been away from his beloved Louisiana and family, the only thing that had kept him willing to go along with being drafted to fight, was getting back to the life he had planned for himself. This first wife must have been beautiful or sweet or some such adjective that would make a man misty eyed when he talked about her, even many years later, during a summer when he and I were working the land together.

He told me that when he first realized that this first wife no longer loved him, he felt hurt, like he had never felt hurt before. It was the type of hurt that ran deep and long; the type that grew inside him; the type that you couldn't just put salve on to make it better. His description of the end always draws my father just a nudge closer to my heart. He said,

> When I came home, I told her that she didn't know what I had been doin', and I didn't know what she had been doin', so we should just forget all that and start back living like we were before I left. But I reckon she didn't like that none, cause after that, she tried to kill me. She put strychnine in my food. But God was on my side, and he saved me. So, she went on to the fair that same day, and I come along and see'd her huggin' and laughin' with another fella. I went over there, and boy they took off. She went one way and he went the other. She didn't even want to see me after that. So, I told her sister that she better not come back to that house, and she didn't. A month later she come up to me at church and asked if she could come get her things. I told her yeah, come on. I was stayin' on ol' Thad Miller's property then, and when he heared tell my wife was coming, he thought for sho' there was gon' be trouble. When my wife come up ol' man Miller come, too; he sat over by the fire with his shotgun in his hand. But they wadn't no trouble. We divided everything up nice, and she took this, and I took that. That old white man just looked at us, and say he ain't never seen nobody get sep'rated like that.

After my father divorced his first wife, he moved back to his parents' house. And there he was once again, under his parents' will. The apples and pomegranates and peaches still needed to be picked for his mother, and his father was still a man who loved to drink almost as much as he loved his wife, Louvenia. There weren't a lot of jobs, and blacks still worked the field, unless they knew some type of trade. No one was going to hire my father as a cook, which is what he'd done in the army, no matter how good he could cook white beans. Cooking was a woman's job; and besides, a strong, young black man was needed to plow somebody's field or even to pick somebody's cotton, he said.

That was when my father chose to work for his father, who also worked for the white landowners in the area. They, the white landowners, respected my father's father—Bob, they called him, though his name was Robert. They knew my grandfather to be a hard worker. They also knew that he raised boys (and girls) who knew how to work. Sometimes, the white neighbors called on Bob to send his children for cotton picking. My father, or Buddy Boy as they called him, was always asked to come. The oldest son, Dutch was married (to Ruth, my mother's sister) and he came, like the ones who were still living at home came. Soon the girls—Bernice, Harriet, Ethel, and Marie—would be married and sharing the lives of their husbands. Jake, one my father's younger brothers, wanted to marry and plow his own land. There weren't a lot of black families, not ones that lived within walking distance, and few people owned cars or trucks. So, Jake married Ruth's younger sister, Mary, one of the few black women, or men, in the area to receive her high school diploma.

Somehow, it wasn't a big surprise that my father would marry the last of the Nickolson girls, my mother, JoeAnna, sister to Ruth and Mary. My father and his brother, Jake, would go on double dates in my Uncle Jake's truck, and because my mother's sister, Mary, wanted to sit next to Jake, my father would sit next to the door on the passenger side.

"This was all right with me," my father said, "because that meant JoeAnna would have to sit in my lap, and I would do anything I could to have her that close to me."

Usually he would show up to court my mother, and her father, a strict deacon and leader in the church, would sit in his chair and watch and listen to my mother and father's conversation. As an already divorced man who was practically thirty years old, my father felt a small twinge of disrespect and dishonor from his soon to be father-in-law. And although my mother was considered used goods, having already birthed a baby girl named Willie Vern out of wedlock (at the age of 13), my mother's father wanted my father to know that "the cow still wasn't for free." My mother's father loved his baby daughter, and though she had brought much embarrassment on his house, he refused to stop treating her like the special child that she was.

People always say that you give what you get, and there is no wonder that my mother was able to overcome her youthful indiscretions, and grow into a woman who knew how to forgive and forget and move on. She would need these valuable and rare qualities during her fifty-three years of marriage to my father.

My father maintains that he loved my mother from the beginning. "That's why I married her on Valentine's Day," he insists. But somewhere after the vows, which he quickly took in the middle of a workday because he had to get back to the fields, he seemed to have accepted that a large chunk of his heart would be closed off, so that my mother could not hurt him the way his first wife had. After his separation from his first wife, he had begun to drink and pick up other bad habits. Prior to that, he told me that he didn't even want to see a bottle of alcohol. He was so strict that if he saw a beer bottle on the side of the road as he was walking by, he would have to stop and push it out of sight.

My mother and father moved to Baton Rouge to find work and an existence that didn't require working from sunup to sundown. Shortly afterwards, they lost their first child—a girl named Anna, who died a heady crib death. Then year after year passed, and it seemed as though my mother would have no more babies. I know that my father always loved children. When he saw his first grandbaby many years later, he would say, "I wonder if her mother will give me that baby." The idea of not being a father could have turned my father and his already cooling heart into a vapid, barely caring human being. I've often heard the old people say, "Don't give up too soon, you never know what's waiting for you around the next corner." That statement is both true and understated because when my mother did begin to conceive children (after she and my father moved back to Sunny Hill to be near her parents), she didn't stop until her body grew weak from heart trouble, and she couldn't produce anymore. All of the remaining nine children that were born lived to be adults.

The talks between my father and me went on and on over those weeks in 2002, just after my mother's death, as he and I worked the old Dyson place.

There was an aluminum swing gate across the road that led up to an old 19th century house, and the owners had gladly given my father the key to the gate so that we could come and go as we needed in completing the job we were hired to do. "Just clean around the trees," the owner's son-in-law—a city boy from Baton Rouge—had told my father.

As soon as we drove up on the first day, I knew why we had been asked to come. There along the edges of the road that started at the gate and ended about five hundred yards when it reached the house, was a line of beautiful old oak trees on each side, but you couldn't truly see the trees themselves—all their aged magnificence was being blocked by an undergrowth, which was slowing taking them over.

"He wants us to clear around these trees," my father said. "And when we finish this, we can start around the sides and back of the house; the old lady wants to be able to see down across them fields."

And beautiful fields they were. In the summer, the landowners always plant hay, and just before the hay is harvested, the green, swaying grass is so breathtaking that only the green of the poinsettia, in the wintertime, eclipses it. The poinsettia's green is rich and bold and full of itself. The green ripens just before the leaves turn a flawless and consummate red. The greenness is indomitable, with multi-stirring veins that course through the leaves like life itself, each perfect in its daring individuality. The green hay fields that greeted us on those first weeks of work reminded me of the poinsettia's life-giving green. Sometimes my father and I would stop with the chopping or sawing or dragging away of limbs and vines, and we would look back on what we had accomplished. For some reason, the sunny fields looked even greener as they sloped ever downward and back up again.

One day, my father and I started to sing my mother's favorite hymn:

> Father I stretch my hands to thee,
> No other help I know.
> If thou withdraw thyself from me,
> Oh, whither shall I go?"[1]

It was something about us singing my mother's hymn (as we called it), our voices carrying across the open fields.

Sometimes, as we worked, I felt that I could see people standing beyond the waves of small hills, especially after my father implicitly declared that these were cotton-picking fields. And when the saw's chain snapped

---

1. Wesley, "Father I Stretch My Hands to Thee."

off, or we simply took a water break, or were too tired to move on, we would stand with our hands resting on the near back of our hips and we would watch the pecan trees and the oak trees that seemed to have just stopped wherever they were and planted themselves. The trees sashayed themselves down through the fields. Some stood like I knew my ancestors had stood: proud, with their legs planted and their tops bending and reaching, bending and reaching until their days were all gone.

One day, I said to my father, "I wonder how many people died in these fields." But he didn't want to talk about stuff like that, he always said. Back in the old days, people worked because they had to, because they had to put food on the table, and because they knew the work had to be done.

"Wadn't nobody else go'n to do it," he said. My father seemed to be talking for all the people who had come before us, who had perhaps worked those fields or fields just like them—some who had no choice, some who did. He seemed to be doing the forgiving for those who wanted it; to be letting go of all that hatred that may have been stored up and locked into the memory of those trees.

My father and I worked the old Dyson place for almost two months, every day gathering our tools and driving over, and every day filled with pride and joy at each inch of brush that we cleared. By the end of the summer, when we drove up, the trees that lined the roadway seemed to smile back, and stand taller, and wave their limbs just a little easier.

At that point, we weren't working for just the money. It was about the nature of life. It was about giving back, taking care of, and thinking not of self. Near the end, the old lady of the house came from Baton Rouge to visit her old treasured homestead. When we drove up and saw her sitting on the garrey (porch), rocking back and forth, with her eyes frolicking somewhere down across the way, we knew our job was over. There were a few more trees to clear, but the job itself had been completed.

What I remember most about that summer was that it became one of the most spiritual times of my life. Giving of one's self, I found, takes commitment and nerve. It is a soul-searching endeavor that cannot be undertaken by those who truly can't let go of the past. It takes hard work. But more than that, it takes forgiveness. Every day as my father and I worked together, side by side and shoulder to shoulder, I grew closer and closer to him. As he talked, I listened. No one is perfect was the gist of it. We all make mistakes that rarely go unnoticed. And somehow, it's usually the people we love the most who get snared in those mistakes.

Being with my father made me constantly think of my mother, for in their last days they had grown so close that you could not see one without the other being close by. I realized that if my mother had not been so extraordinarily special, my father may not have paled by comparison, and that he possibly did pale comparatively because he had no choice. I thought about my mother's funeral, and how the people came. They really came. Black and white people came. Old and new friends came. High ranking dignitaries came and lowly people off the streets came. And the Solid Rock Male Chorus sang and praised with Keith Long and Jackie Huff and my cousin Rosetta; and the people who stood talked about how much she would be missed; and we all tried to stop the tears for those few hours, as we celebrated her life. When I saw my father being dragged in, almost carried in by my brothers, everything seemed like the beginning of death for him. My father, even at 82 years of life then, was vital and physically strong. Yet, he faltered, like he would falter for the next six and a half years after losing his wife. Loss. He came to understand his great, great loss.

The Chicken Hawk

The thing that truly fascinated my father and me on this particular morning was a bird—a bird that at first seemed large and menacing to us. As we drove half way up the four hundred-foot driveway of the old house, we pulled our small truck over, along the edge of the country road, and got out. Generally, my father would go directly to the back of the truck and begin taking out our tools, but on this morning he marveled at the progress we'd made over the past weeks. He stood with his hands locked firmly on his back and stretched himself out like one of the tall, lean trees. I began to share in his moment of appreciation, and indeed, the scene almost took my breath away. Behind us, on each side of the road was a line of aged oaks (and an occasional pecan or pine tree) that was no longer hidden by brush. We had cleared the brush away, slowly, each day inching our way along the tree-lined roadway. Now, we could look at each tree, from the bottom of its exposed trunk to the top of high and elongated limbs that waved peacefully in our direction. Through the trees we could see beyond the fields—fields that seemed to gather in little crevices of darker, richer greenness against the clear blue brightness of the sky. *Little hills and valleys of color*, my father and I always said. On this morning, our eyes moved back toward us, along the edges, picking up the beauty of the moment. Suddenly, as if from nowhere, or as if it had been magically planted there, appeared the large bird.

"Look," I said to my father, who stood just a few feet away from me.

His head turned, and I could almost feel his eyes land on the bird. He was startled somewhat, just enough to make his body twitch, before he was himself again.

THE CHICKEN HAWK

"Looky there," was all he could say.

We stood there staring at the bird, and it stood staring at us. Its eyes seemed coated slightly. This I could see from the twenty or so feet that separated us from the animal.

"What kind of bird is it?" I asked my father, figuring that he would know since there weren't too many things he didn't know about animals, wild or not. He had often kept wild pets over the years. Once, when I was very young, and much to my mother's disapproval, he had even raised a rooster in our house. The rooster stayed perched on my father's favorite chair, a recliner that none of us were allowed to sit in. Actually, after the rooster came to call it home, none of us wanted to sit in the chair. Every day my father would have to clean rooster poop from the seat even before *he* could sit down.

"Looks like some kind of hawk," my father finally said, after much thought. "Prob'ly a chicken hawk, but the color's a little off. And they don't use'ly take kindly to humans."

The hawk, as we mentally decided to label it, continued to monitor us without moving even an eye or twitching a feather. I thought back to my childhood when we had first moved to our second house. Because we had so much more land than before, my parents had greedily grabbed at the idea of a farm in the true sense—not like the dairy farm we had always lived on. Every imaginable animal was accounted for. At one point, our chicken coop boasted hundreds of chickens. Sometimes the chickens would smarten up and find a way out of the coop and then, usually in the early afternoons, if we children were outside, we'd hear the unmistakable sounds of a chicken hawk having flown down and snatched up one of those straying chickens—the chicken would screech and flap its wings, and cry out for help that would not come. It was an amazing thing to see. My brother David, when he had turned a teenager, took to shooting at the hawks, and once or twice succeeding in killing one. He had proudly shown it off to our neighboring buddies, but I thought it was a waste. There the large, beautiful bird would lie in his hands, lifeless—its large beak magnificent, with claws that seemed capable of overcoming even the old man roosters on the farm. We hated those roosters because they weren't afraid of anything or anyone, even us. I always felt my brother was getting rid of the wrong animals.

The particular hawk that my father and I found on that morning barely resembled the chicken hawks of my youth. This one was mostly a rich caramel brown, with much darker wings. Its head was darkest of all, like an eagle's. In my heart, I wished it were an eagle. I'm not sure why. Perhaps I wanted to assign some great purpose to the bird's life, for instinctively I knew it was ill, that perhaps it had come to this beautiful place that my father and I were reviving, to die. Perhaps I needed a reason to care about the animal's fate. And yet, it held the stigma of chicken hawks—killers of smaller birds—and I had never understood this, to be frank. I couldn't understand any animal that hurt its own kind. Perhaps I had simply remembered chicken hawks as meaner and tougher, more vibrant and more capable. This one sat there on the ground, gingerly on its hind legs.

My father didn't know what to say or do about it. After several minutes of perusing the hawk's interests, we decided to get to work. The sun had already come up, and soon it would be too hot for labor. That was when my father decided to talk to the hawk, as he was often wont to do in the old days when he kept animals.

"You may be crippled or not," my father said. "Either way, show look like you need our help."

I looked at the hawk and it looked at me: as if we both wondered how my father had come to this conclusion. My father simply continued to speak to hawk, as though they had suddenly become great friends.

"Looky here," my father said as he pointed one of his knotty, black hands at the hawk. "Now, we got some work to do. We gon' try and make our way further up this roadside, but when we get done, I'll come back and check on you. I think you may need help, so I tell you what: you be down here by this truck when we get ready to go and I'll take you with me. You'll come stay with me. Now, that's all I 'tend to say on the subject."

With that, my father and I gathered the chain saw, the rake and hoe, the limb trimmer, and a jug of ice water, and left the hawk to its own peace. We moved to the opposite side of the road where we worked for a few hours. During the course of the morning, we mostly forgot about the hawk, for our work was hard and difficult. I often watched my 82 year old father, and I marveled at how effortlessly he moved alongside me. I had always been athletic, playing basketball throughout my life, and those years of working the fields as a child had taught me, conditioned and sustained me to work long and hard. In my adult years, I often noticed people in other parts of the country and world who hadn't been raised with my same work ethic, who didn't seem to have the same work stamina. I had noticed because it was always so obvious. My parents had often said when we were children that we should be able to work as well physically as mentally. As my father

THE CHICKEN HAWK

and I worked that summer, alongside each other, neither getting exhausted until the afternoon sun rose too high and too heavily in the sky, that was when I truly realized the value of what my parents had said. As I watched my father, his age not the slightest barrier in his desire to work and remain productive, I knew that hard work was not a bad thing.

Once or twice during the morning, the chain slipped off the chain saw and I went back to the truck to reposition it, as well as to add oil and gas to the saw. On one of these breaks, I noticed that the hawk had moved. Not far away from the spot where we had first seen it, but I formed a growing hope that the hawk was okay, that it was moving away to take care of itself. I began to think that it had simply stopped, purposefully, to meet my father and me on that day. That the hawk was not hurt, but was resting, watching us, getting to know us from afar, before it took off again and journeyed onward. Those were nice thoughts that entertained me when by chance I'd glance over at the hawk, which remained sitting along the edge of the green meadow.

At the end of the little trips that I made to the truck, I would report to my father the hawk's movements. "It has moved slightly away," I said once. "The hawk is still there," I said on another occasion. "I believe he wants to take flight," I said later. "I believe I saw it checking its wings, Daddy."

At these pronouncements my father smiled and grinned, for the idea of the hawk had now engrossed his heart, and I could see that when we were done, he'd want the bird to be there waiting for him. I could already see my father taking the hawk home with him. I could see the pen that he would build for this brave animal. I could see the gentle way my father would behave with this hawk: it would be a precious object that only he could handle. I could see all of that and more; the truth was that I wanted it for my father. As I said, both his heart and mine had been sliced into pieces by then. We both still cried and talked sadly about how much we missed my mother, who had died the year before. My father told me that on some nights he would awaken and feel justified in simply sitting at the edge of the bed and talking to his dead wife, just as he had done for all the fifty-three years of their lives together.

Every time we both went to church, we agreed it was the place that hurt us the most, for it was there that she was still so present, still such a reminder of the person we both missed so much. She had sat in the Amen corner, sending out shouts of support to my father when he was in the pulpit.

I said to my father, often, that summer, "I thought we would lose you too, Daddy." At the funeral, he had been almost carried into the church by my brothers. He had sat there for the entire funeral, looking lost and wearied, barely making a movement, his eyes filled with tears at the loss of his wife. We all thought he had given up and would prove that the old saying was true: A person who'd been married so many years couldn't last for very long after the other spouse had passed away.

Talking with my father, listening to him as we worked, gave me new perspective on how much he was suffering. Perhaps that was when I began to see and notice the gross amounts of anger that came from me. How could someone who had been such a terrible husband hurt as much as my father did then? That was what I wanted to know. My question at times, struck out at him like a weapon intent on destroying his resolve, his comfort in living. He once told me that neither he nor my mother had been perfect in their marriage. This angered me further. I stood there with the small chain saw in my hands, ready to rip on the cord to start it, but I hesitated because I knew that I might literally strike out at him and cut into pieces what remained of this man, this man who was my father, this man who was trying to help me make sense of the way he'd lived his life with my mother. All I could remember were the fights, the disrespect of all his mistresses, the coming home in the early morning hours, and the mistreatment of his stepdaughter. I placed the saw on the ground, then picked up the hoe and began chopping viciously at the small weeds on the ground.

At around 1:00 p.m., my father and I had drunk most of the water, leaving the rest of it hot and iceless. The sun beat down on us even through the covering blanket of the trees, so we decided to call it a day. We knew we would be back the next day to pick up where we'd left off. We gathered the tools and raked up around the area where we had worked, making even clearer tracks around the trees, and then headed back to the truck. As soon as we reached the back, we both almost dropped the tools we were carrying because there, about ten feet from the tailgate of the truck, sat the hawk—the one that my father had befriended, had talked to and told to be there when we returned at the end of our workday.

We stopped our movement forward, not wanting to frighten the bird away, but the longer we stood there and it remained, we realized that the hawk didn't plan on leaving us. We placed our saw and other tools onto the truck, took off our gloves and tossed them on top of the pile, and then gave our full attention to the animal.

THE CHICKEN HAWK

My father said to me, almost in a whisper, "I'd done almost forgot about him."

"Yeah, me, too," I assured him. We had worked an hour since I had last looked for the hawk.

"Well, that settles it," my father said.

"What's that, Daddy?"

"Well, I told him if he was here when we got ready to go, I'd take him with me. I guess he want to go."

At this point, I didn't question my father's resolve to take the hawk because how could I doubt what he said was true. There, you see, was the proof—the bird sat waiting, as though it had packed its bags and was ready to go on this trip with us, perhaps the trip of its large and generally unfettered life.

Slowly, my father began to walk toward the hawk. With every step that he made, he stopped, giving it the chance to flee. The hawk made no movements; it sat there watching my father's progress. My father moved so slowly, so intently, that soon I thought the ailing bird would topple over while waiting for my father to get there; for by now, we could see that the bird's broad and brown-patched chest had slumped down. Its head sat lower as well, as though it were now praying—praying for something to be done.

I wanted to tell my father to put his gloves back on, in case the hawk decided to peck at him with its large, deadly beak. My father seemed intent on doing things his way, so I remained quiet and waited for whatever would happen.

My father kneeled down as he held out his hand, offering it to the animal. The hawk turned its head to look directly at my father, but made no other movements. My father's arm remained there for a minute, as he waited, hoping the bird would climb aboard.

"Perhaps it's too weak, Daddy." I said this softly to my father.

Without saying a word, my father simply stood half way up and then reached down with both hands and lifted the hawk at the base of its wings. The hawk seemed to melt into my father's hands, as though my father and it had indeed been lifelong friends. A small cry came from the bird. It was nothing like the strong squawking of the chicken hawks that I remembered from my youth. The helplessness of the mighty creature was so apparent at that moment. My father gently walked the hawk over to the tailgate of the truck and sat it down. He began to look it over, lifting its wings, feeling around its thick legs, rubbing across its great head. The bird allowed my father to do this; it did not wrestle about or try to stop my father in any way.

This familiarity that the animal had with my father was touching for me to see. It reminded me of all my father's great qualities, all the things that had endeared him to me over the years. It made me want to be closer to him, to join him in becoming one with this moment. Neither of us was afraid of the large hawk, which now sat upon the bed of the truck like a powerful block of feathers and force. I moved next to my father, searching with him for signs of the hawk's ailment. We could find none. My father surmised that the hawk was suffering from something it had eaten, perhaps a diseased animal. "Or," he said, "could be, it's his time to go, and he don't want to leave this world alone."

After a while of perusing the hawk's interests, my father and I decided to take it with us, to try to find a refuge for it, or to take it to a veterinarian for treatment. We cleared a spot on the truck for the hawk to sit comfortably, placed an old sack on the spot, and then placed the bird upon the bedding. When we got home, which was only a few minutes away, we began calling around the entire state of Louisiana trying to find a bird refuge or any other bird rescue operation that might take the animal. We could find none. The closest we came was the Audubon Zoo in New Orleans, which was just over an hour's drive. We had already agreed that we would see the hawk to its next habitat, so the distance did not concern us. A zoo representative told us that perhaps the aquarium might take the bird (the aquarium's Mississippi exhibit had a number of rescued birds on display), but after we waited for more than twenty minutes on hold, we were told that the aquarium wasn't taking any more birds at that time.

We had been calling around for well over an hour and this latest news deflated my father's ego and spirit, and mine as well. At no time had we thought we wouldn't succeed in this endeavor to save the hawk's life. We had called several veterinarians and animal hospitals around the area surrounding New Orleans, and none of them had wanted to take the animal either. I could see that my father was getting weary of the whole affair. He had taken several trips to the truck to check on the hawk, and after so many calls and so many letdowns, my father began to wonder what would happen to the bird. He seemed to understand that he could not take care of the hawk, that what ailed it was greater than his human powers could manage.

A veterinarian in Bogalusa agreed to look at the bird, and suddenly, we were rushing about, gathering our belongings, making ready for the next journey of the hawk's life. Before we pulled away, we removed our tools and placed the hawk in a position closer to the cab of the truck, so that it would be protected from the wind. We opened the window at the back of the truck, and as I drove along, my father would reach back and check on the hawk's condition. The hawk remained leaning against the truck, staring off vaguely. I felt as though this great animal understood the measures we were taking on its behalf.

As soon as we pulled into the parking lot of the veterinarian's office, my father jumped from the truck and rushed into the facility. Moments later, two young women, wearing white coats that had been dirtied by their particular job, came to the truck and examined the hawk. "Yes, it does look like a chicken hawk," one of them said. The other one gathered up the bird, holding it close to her chest as she went swiftly into the building. My father and I followed, anxious to know the hawk's prognosis.

After many minutes, which seemed like hours, one of the young women came out and said that because the veterinarian was not on the premises, there was little she and her associate could do. She allowed us to leave our phone number so that she could call us with any news on the hawk.

Several days passed and my father and I didn't hear from this veterinarian, so we called, no longer able to withstand the suspense of not knowing. I dialed the number for my father and then gave him the phone because I knew he would want to talk to the veterinarian himself.

"Yes . . . Unh hunh . . . yes," I heard my father say, as he listened to the news. When he hung up the phone, I asked him what had happened. I could already see the sadness in his eyes, and I guessed the outcome.

"It didn't make it," he said. "We was too late."

"They couldn't help it?"

"It was on its last leg when we got it . . . just waiting to die, prob'ly."

"What'd it die of," I asked. I figured there must be some explanation other than it was the hawk's time to die.

"They don't know," my father said. "The girl said they didn't have the 'sources to do a autopsy. 'Specially since its just some chicken hawk, I guess."

"Yeah," I agreed.

Our hearts melted a little more about the hawk, as about life and death in general. We wanted answers to these age-old questions of why things like this happen. My father and I were sad for the rest of that day. As I said, we had truly thought we would save the hawk's life. The thought of it had made us feel godly for a while, had given us hope in the grand scheme of things, had offered us a brief, if illusory, explanation for why we had been planted here on earth. Like saving the hawk might save us as well.

The next day, when we went back to work, we left home without any type of anticipation. Not even the beauty of the land impressed us on that morning as we opened the gates and drove onto the stunning spaciousness of the land. The cleared trees, standing tall, their trunks bared to us, like their souls were on display, did not spark within our hearts the usual glee and love of all that is nature. As we drove past the spot where we had first discovered the hawk sitting, waiting for us to take it away with us, my father and I looked upon the scene as though we had been accomplices in this animal's demise.

We gathered our tools and went to work without speaking to the other. Silently, much of the morning went away from us as we worked side-by-side, pulling and cutting on the vegetative debris. Our disgust at the world made our strength even greater and we pulled easily at the weeds that came gripping from the earth. The small limbs and trees seemed lighter and less tough against our full-bodied anger. And when we perchance glanced over at the spot where the bird had sat waiting for us on that morning, our strength grew even greater than before. We worked with nothing but fierceness that morning.

But as the days went on, and each morning came and went, even as we came and went, clearing the ugliness away from the beauty of the land, my father and I came to appreciate the small distraction of the hawk's visit. We began to look upon the spot where the bird had sat as a special place. The spot became sacred to us, for it began to represent something more. It came to represent the few hours we had had to reflect on something other than my mother's passing. It had taken us away from the grief of our daily existence and had offered a few moments of respite, a few moments to judge life on terms other than what we had lost.

A few weeks after we found the hawk, my father told the story in the pulpit, during a sermon. He told the congregation that sometimes we, as humans, need help and we don't know how to ask for it. "The hawk," he said, "needed help. The only way he knew how to get it was to wait there by the truck for me when I returned. 'Be there by that truck when I get back,' I told him, and he was. That's the same way we have to live as Christians: when you need help, don't be afraid to ask for it. Don't be afraid to wait there by the truck if you have to and wait on the Lord. He will always send someone willing to lend a hand."

What could I say to that? Once again, my father had reminded me of why I loved him, and at least momentarily, why the wrongs of his past did not outweigh the basic and overriding love I felt for him. As I sat there on the church pew, listening to my father, I marveled at how a small yet desperate visit from a chicken hawk had given my father and me a few moments of peace.

Living Spaces

Most of us take for granted that we will have a decent, respectable place to live; after all, isn't this our God-given right, if not as citizens of this great nation, then certainly as civilized beings of earth? The truth is that we *do* deserve it—the fact is that we *don't* always get it.

I once had a friend who went to live with her new husband in the tiniest of mobile homes that had ever been built. She and I were in the navy, stationed near Big Sur, California, and, until she got married, we had shared a room in the barracks on base. I encouraged her to go, *be with her man*, even to marry him—not because I was all that concerned about her immanent happiness, but because I greedily wanted the room all to myself. It would be the first and only time in my life that I had an individual place to stay. For other reasons as well, but I had taken up the hobby of growing flowers then, and her presence, I told myself, was constricting to their growth. The flowers and I needed to stretch out, my young mind surmised. I also told myself that she loved this man beyond sense. At last, when she walked out of this room that was now all mine—that I had mortgaged with a little of my soul—I smiled with my friend and gave her the warmest embrace, as though I had stored all my compassion up for just that occasion. The truth was that I had plenty to spare.

When we were children, the first house we lived in was too small for all the people who lived there. Along with my cousin Eddie, there were eight siblings then, sleeping two or three to a bed since there was only a few small bedrooms in the house. We didn't particularly like it, and yet we thought, *this must be one of those inconveniences that children must endure.* It was in those days. We all understood that the more sisters and brothers one had, the less room there was for sleeping. We adapted willingly enough, particularly when our cousins came to visit and we sometimes slept up to six children in a twin-sized bed. Again, we didn't seem to mind. We'd spend the night laughing and tickling and giggling as quietly as we could, lest my mother come in and spank us all. When the morning came, it wasn't unusual to find idle arms and legs suffocating the smallest and most vulnerable, as well as fingers and toes digging into each other's bellies and armpits.

One would think that the worst thing about living in New Orleans after Katrina was that every single element of life seemed overturned and stuck in disarray. There wasn't one worst thing: all of it sat equal in our gigantic room of altered life. *Their needs must be specific though,* we heard so many outsiders say. *You need a plan,* those at the top reminded us. Even those of us who lived here in the immediate months wanted to know why the wheels of normalcy would not turn. Like a bell ringing, we'd be reminded when we drove by a house with half a roof and a tiny FEMA trailer in the driveway. Or when we saw on TV that people were stealing propane canisters if they weren't chained and locked to the front of the trailers. These opportunistic thieves weren't necessarily stealing the canisters for profit, but because there was a shortage. We'd think of the looters, who months before stole clothes and food to survive. We'd wonder if it would ever end. We'd listen to the radio and hear story after story about people who still had not received a FEMA trailer, who still had no place to live. In the old, pre-Katrina days, we might have said, *It's only a mobile home, for God's sake. Where is your self-respect?*

At the barracks, word finally got out that my old roommate was living practically in squalor. *That trailer is too small for even one person to live in,* all the friends and whisperers said. I refused to believe it though. How small could it be, I reasoned. Who would choose to go live somewhere that was too small? Hadn't they shared many nights together in just this place long before the marital knot was tied? Instead of wondering if my friends were right, I put it out of my mind and continued to enjoy the pleasures of living alone. Every morning, I woke to the sound of my own alarm. I dressed when I pleased, throwing off my robe with ease, ironing then putting on my uniform within plenty of time to make muster. I toasted bread and drank chocolate milk that was no longer missing from the refrigerator. All of my belongings were finally mine and only mine. And every morning, just before I walked out the door to go to work, I watered my beautiful plants, quite certain and sure that they were the happiest vegetation on earth. I went about my day, not once thinking about the living conditions I had helped my friend place herself in.

The day remains in my memory, all these years later. I see all of us kids on the back of my father's truck, wondering what was going on. Our parents didn't tell us much about those kinds of things. A quick, *We're going to be moving*, was all they could share. Then there were the houses we were supposedly interested in; we would visit these empty houses and decide later whether we wanted to live in one of them. At each, we jumped off the back of the truck and systematically rummaged through the empty dwellings as though we could afford them, as though we would actually buy a house. Even the youngest of us kids knew that my father's credit was the worst thing about him. But there we all were, and the nonsense of it showed on my mother's face. She had no smiles to give. My father rushed us back on the truck after each house had been trampled through and summed up. He did this with the same joking spirit he always relied on to get through life. *How lucky these neighbor people will be to have us live here,* he said. At one of the houses, there was a front porch that sat low to the ground. Each child was already dreaming about all the fun we'd have jumping over the small wall that enclosed the porch. At another house, we cringed at the thought of living in a house that was hidden by a large man-made embankment. *I can't see the road*, I said to my mother. *Me neither, child*, she returned. All I'm saying, all these years later, is that it was no surprise when we didn't move into any of those houses.

The people of New Orleans seemed to come back in halfsies, so many of them broken apart by Katrina's hard hands. The people's hearts and minds and all their internals were there, but just beneath the surface, they were barely functioning. The looks on their faces would sometimes haunt me into my evening hour, and into my dreams. One night, I dreamed of a man returning home, as though he had been living on the open plains, and when he returned home, there instead of his house was a yellowed glob of mud spread out over the ground, thick and obviously meant to replace what once was his home. I saw his son, quite like the man—both stood looking about in wonder. I knew they would find no answer, so I left them standing there.

Mostly, conversations about FEMA caught my ear:

"They said my trailer would be here a month ago and I still haven't seen it."

"No, listen to this, FEMA tried to give my neighbor over twenty thousand dollars and they didn't even have half that damage. My neighbor told them to keep that money and give it to someone who needed it."

"Humph, your neighbor sure was crazy. I'm getting all I can from FEMA 'cause the government sure done got plenty from me!"

"Me, too, girl. Them crazies at FEMA messed up our paperwork and brought us two trailers. You think we told 'em about it? Sure didn't."

"My grandmother's house was covered in nine feet of water and FEMA told her she didn't qualify for a trailer."

Someone else latches on to the conversation: "Why all y'all sittin' around waitin' on FEMA? God gave you hands; you better git to using them!"

"Sound like somebody with plenty of money, honey."

"Girl, you ain't never lied."

"I don't know what she talking about anyway. I know rich folks *and* poor folks living in FEMA trailers. What else they gonna stay in?"

"Now, that's the truth. I saw one over the Christmas holidays that was all lit up, decorated so nice like. Who got enough gumption to throw some lights on a FEMA trailer"?

"I don't know what you mean. I think it's a little of heaven smiling down on all of us."

"Yes, Lord, you may be right. I was thinking about giving mine a name."

High fives all around.

"You, too? I saw somebody named theirs the Creole Queen."

"You know this still the Big Easy; people just take whatever happen and figure out a way to keep going. They ain't no mo' worried about tomorrow than yesterday is."

"Yeah, you right."

When curiosity could no longer sustain me, I made the trip to see my friend and her husband in their small home. It was located in a trailer park near

Big Sur. As I turned off the roadway, I saw what appeared to be a giant egg lost in the woods. The egg was nestled beneath aged redwoods that towered, leaning on the sky. There were so many trees that a light dusk covered the base of the park. The closer I got, I recognized my friend's car, which looked frighteningly larger than the egg trailer. Getting out of my little Chevy, I could hear them moving, bumping around inside. Their movements made the trailer shake and slightly scrape against one of the redwoods. I knocked, and there was silence. For a moment, I thought they would try to pretend they weren't home. Then the door swung open, so wide that it slammed against the outside of the chalky white trailer. They invited me in, joyously. Their eyes said, *The main course has finally arrived*. Ducking my head, I went on in, slowly.

There were piles of clothes everywhere. All the clothes my former roommate had packed were now strewn about the cabin-like structure. I couldn't get comfortable, couldn't stand completely up, couldn't look beyond a few feet before my eyes were forced to turn in a different direction. The small bed hung over a kitchen table that folded out from a seat that spanned the front of their home. The stove wasn't a stove but a counter with a butane hookup. There was a small curtain that appeared to hide some type of doorway. I was told that this was the bathroom. Peeking in, the toilet was even chintzier than those I'd seen on airplanes, and there was no bathtub or shower at all. *We go to the clubhouse over there for our showers*, she told me. After the unlengthy tour, there was small talk. The *how-you-beens* lasted exactly one minute. The *what-you-doing-these-days* lasted only a minute longer. It wasn't that they didn't want to talk; it was me. The guilt was shutting me up. I couldn't even stumble on a word to say.

Our family was eventually tasked with moving away from our first house. My memory of it is that we stole away in the middle of the night, like people who are on the run, trying to escape to freedom. Only we were already free, and we weren't escaping to a better place. The house that we would move into was ill-prepared for us. At first, there was no indoor bathroom and no running water. It was as though some ancient peoples had lived there prior to us and had left the house to manage on its own—with nary a family or friend or foe to come and buff it into shape before we moved in. The whole experience was a shock to our systems, to be living so. That's when I learned that even children can be particular when they want to be. We begged to go back to our old, modern house. My mother gave us a look that said, *Don't you know we would if we could.* The new man who owned the property that we had been living on would not hear of it. My father would not hear of it. No matter what happened to us, we were not going back to our house.

The people of New Orleans wanted to come home (many of them are still trying to get home). I know this as surely as I know the day is brighter than night. I remember all the years I spent traveling across the world, and at no time did I ever think of never coming home. I knew I would find my way back to Louisiana. One misses the familiarities, the candid way life overtakes yet leaves one feeling fine just the same. There was always a gentle call to return home: the way people talked, laughed, played, prayed, all the things that made sense. Even the doubts reminded me when it was time to come home.

As Fortunes Go

Boethius said, "*In omni adversitate fortunae infelicissimum est genus in fortunii fuisse felicem*" (or, it is a most miserable fortune to have once been happy).[1] Sitting home alone on New Year's Eve, 2006, when so many New Orleanians have not returned to the city yet, my mind wanders. All is mostly quiet beyond my walls, with the exception of a few firecrackers exploding in the distance. In moments like these, it's the missing people that I long for the most.

It makes me think of life and death: we speak as though these are two separate entities. I wonder if it's not all about life, and death, just a sore part of it—like a child who waits around to get her way. If we are lucky, death is only a small part of it, just the *denouement*, as it were. There are only other deaths to lament—deaths that come when we've been lucky enough to have known people in our lives worth missing. Only then does death matter; only then does it become Somebody.

Writing is about the walks and paths that will lead to my final resting place.

When I'm talking to my father, he rarely speaks about the troubles and misery he surely endured as a child growing up in depression era America, or as a man who lived through eighty years of the twentieth century. He doesn't remember the worst of it, only that his mother and father loved him enough to beat some sense into him. When I look into his eyes, I know that he wonders if it was enough.

1. Boethius, *The Consolation of Philosophy*, 524.

I often dream about how I could replace grief with love. Boccaccio said, "Love is mightier than destiny."[2] Shouldn't it *be* destiny?

After my father united all his children, both from his union with my mother and from the affair he had with the Tabor woman, he was then happy—never mind that my mother was dead, not alive to see it. On Family and Friend's Day, 2002, all his children showed up at church. Our family, with my father at the helm, actually won first place for the number of family members present. Afterwards, my father said to me, "Well, I know one thing for sure, if they don't want me around here (speaking of our family—the children he had with my mother), I've got somewhere else I know I can go (speaking of this newfound gaggle of children). I knew then that he was thinking about skipping town—taking the easy way out, once again. I closed my ears to him and wished I didn't see all his faults so clearly.

When I was young, my father's brother, Jake, came to our house to buy food stamps from my father. I remember my father standing there by his old Chevy truck. He had on dirty overalls as usual, and had probably come in from the field, either plowing the garden, or putting down some fertilizer or some such farm thing. He and my uncle talked as though they were businessmen, each bargaining for his own profits. At last I heard my father say to my uncle, "Thirty is all I can sell you; you know how many mouths I got to feed."

I heard the beginnings of a conversation outside my window one day:
 "God, you see, always take the good and leave these bad motherfuckers here."
 "Don't you know it, man."
 "I know every good person in my life is gone, but them murderin,' gun-totin' motherfuckers still walking around here."
 "Yeah, don't you know it.

When we were children, our pastor told us a story of how he'd seen an old, haggled looking person on the side of the road, but that he did not stop to help the stranger. His excuse: he didn't like the way the man looked; it was possible that the stranger would have tried to murder him or steal from

---

2. Boccaccio, *The Decameron*, 1353.

him. When we got home from church, my father was almost livid with disdain for our pastor's actions, as was I. (He and I agreed on this.) My father said, "Wouldn't you think a preacher would stop to help the man, even if no one else would?" We were both perplexed by the pastor's obliviousness to another human's needs. We surmised that the pastor was scared of dying. Shouldn't he, of all people, be ready to meet his maker, and with the briefest of notifications? Apparently not. My father added this to the pastor's other *faux pas* or what he deemed lapses in pastorly judgment. Once the pastor had boasted, "There was a time when all I had to eat was red beans and rice for dinner," to which my father said, "I still have to eat red beans and rice for dinner." He seemed perturbed that the pastor wasn't acting like the person he'd set himself up to be: a great and supposedly saved man who understood and could commiserate with other people's suffering. If memory serves me, my father was sitting at the table when he said this, a table where he had often denied the neighbor children a seat for dinner. I looked at him with clear eyes, wondering if he seriously didn't see the contradiction in his own living.

Kierkegaard said, "It is only after a man has thus understood himself inwardly and has thus seen his way, that life acquires peace and significance."[3] I have no words when I read this, just hope.

My mother died on a Friday. Sitting in my apartment alone, I talked to her on the phone not long before she left this world. It becomes more difficult to remember what we talked about in that last conversation. I know that she complained about injustice, and I asked her to stop getting herself upset about things she could not control. The conversation was ordinary otherwise. When we hung up the phone, I knew that life was unfair, yes, but because she was in it, things weren't so bad. I felt for her, that she would always worry for her children, that she would rarely have a day when life would come easily and serendipitously for her. Fifty or so minutes passed, and the phone rang again. It was one of my mother's friends. She didn't ask me to sit down, she simply said, "It's your mother . . . she's dead." Fear overtook me in large doses of adrenaline. Minutes later, emptiness replaced the fear. Grief: the status changer.

---

3. Kierkegaard, *Journals: Search for Personal Meaning*, 1830s.

Recently, I dreamed about a clock ticking. Then I saw French fries and fried fish being cooked in the same grease. I hate that. People don't care about such things anymore. They do believe, though, in love, country, and war with their enemies, no matter how newly formed the bond had been. I want my fries to be soft in the center and somewhat crispy around the edges, but never sprinkled with tiny cornmeal nuggets.

Someone once asked me how I could accept my father's mistakes so easily, especially accept his full-grown gaggle of children from outside the family. I answered that people are human; that doesn't mean you stop loving them. I wonder if I truly meant what I said.

I've often thought that I would write my life into sense, that I would see my clear purpose then. Once, a friend who hasn't a clue about a writer's craft tried to tell me how I should write. She said, "You have to be able to write at a moment's notice." I told her, "That's not the way I write." She said, "You sound like you're some great writer already." And I said, "Well, in my mind I am." She was flabbergasted.

It strikes me that most people don't take the time to get to know you—they form these little lay opinions, obliterate you with them, and then they keep going, on to the next cause that they won't stop for.

A newer meaning of grief: You don't think you deserve good things, and when anything good happens, you dismiss it as a mistake, like a wrong number that you wish you hadn't bothered to answer.

The thing about my mother's death is that I thought, fully, from the most singular to the most collective parts of me, that I would not survive it. I knew personally that my mother had been holding all of us together, even to the detriment of her own life. I knew this was something that she had gladly and most purposefully done for us. And though I felt guilty, I had allowed her to do so.

The end of a conversation I heard outside my window recently:
"What color woman did Moses marry"?
"I don't know, man."

"A black woman, that's who. Started the black race. Yeah man, it's in the Bible."

No reply.

"You know where I get it from? Right here, man." The sounds of reggae music thump thump from the car radio. "It all comes from reggae, man."

Circumstances can either be powerful allies or vicious enemies. People who were given every advantage should not be regarded as superior, just like people who grow up in deplorable situations should not be blamed for all that they did not achieve. And yet we all have choices. Either we continue to grow from that jumping off place we were born into, or we sit around and become static and stagnant, complaining about what others have taken from us, remaining hungry for options for the rest of our lives. I like the idea that Jesus took two fishes and five loaves of bread and fed thousands.

I've always gone back to the country, to the place of my youth, for nourishment. There is something so sweet about those first moments when I arrive "home." I think it's the trees. They stand like friendly sentries, like old mothers, like strength personified. The wind through the trees is a sound that no city dweller can hear, and when I've remained in the city too long, I find that I must listen longer after I cross the big lake. That sound, it has an essence I instinctively understand—it is the faint sound of forgiveness.

Katrina took most of our trees away with her. They say it will take two hundred and fifty years to bring them back to what they were just a few months ago. In those first moments after Katrina hit, when I walked outside and saw with fresh eyes how weird the destruction of life can be, I wanted to cry out for the trees, for all those that would not live again. Most came up by the roots and laid themselves down as though they were sleeping; others, God had reached down and snapped them in two. Walking amongst their dead, I stepped, crawled, or pulled myself over the largest of trunks. Some had held their limbs high, as though they were afraid of drowning.

Kafka said, "In the final analysis writing depends not on vigilance but on the ability to forget one's self." He also said, "A writer who does not write is a monster who positively invokes madness."[4] Until recently, the only thing I could write about was loss, as though I owned the inky pipeline to despair.

---

4. Kafka, *The Diaries of Franz Kafka,* 1910-1913.

I must be able to go where life takes me and then to come back again—it's the only way I will ever be free; it's the only way I can write.

I pick up Edna St. Vincent Millay on this late, late evening, waiting for time to change again, permanently. I never tire of reading these lines:

> It is not enough that yearly, down this hill
> April comes like an idiot, babbling and strewing flowers.[5]

There aren't many more perfect lines. If the "babbling" doesn't awaken some monumental spirit within me, then the "strewing" certainly does. And that we should delight in calling April a beautiful idiot? Yes, we should.

---

5. Millay, "Spring," 1921.

A Daughter Remembers
... Her Father

> Now why is procreation the object of love? Because procreation is the nearest thing to perpetuity and immortality that a mortal being can attain. If, as we agreed, the aim of love is the perpetual possession of the good, it necessarily follows that it must desire immortality together with the good, and the argument leads us to the inevitable conclusion that love is love of immortality as well as of the good.[1]
>
> —PLATO, *SYMPOSIUM*

In early December 2007, my father was rushed to the local hospital. Just in time, the doctors said, for if there had been further delay, they would not have been able to operate and remove the gastric ulcer that sat bubbling in his stomach and tearing his life away.

"It could be cancerous," they then said. Pieces were rushed to the lab, but since this was a small town hospital, the results would not be known

---

1. Plato, *Symposium*, 360 BC.

straight off. My father had been diagnosed with prostate cancer in 1991 and, although such a cancer is often much less of a death sentence, at least right away, his prognosis was not good. He was already seventy-two years old, and the VA doctors thought that surely, he would not live past another few years. He had a younger brother who would, in fact, later be diagnosed with the same disease and would die more quickly.

That December, after my father's surgery, I placed the results of his biopsy out of my mind, as if I did not wish to know the results. I was in the middle of giving final exams—this was clearly an excuse not to have to deal with the inevitable. It took me two days to get to the hospital. This was a problem: he had been asking for me. Somehow he asked for me often since this disease had progressed, even though I was not considered his "favored" child.

I have always written about my father. Even as a child, I would lie in my bed late at night and listen to him stumble into our house and get into yet another argument or knock-each-other-out fight with my mother. As I heard these things happening, I would imagine the scene differently. In this new version that I would write in my head, my father would be just as handsome—his rock solid cheeks, big smile, and caring eyes would never change. His thin body, with arms muscled by the heavy work of dairy farming, would always be capable of lifting me high above his head and swinging me around and around, on those early evenings when he would play with me and my siblings, just before he himself got dressed in his finest clothes and went out into the nightfall—to, we all assumed, play with people his own size.

He would not stumble into the house in this imaginary version of my father's return. He would walk in briskly, smiling, or perhaps laughing, and he would greet my mother, who would be waiting with her arms open. She would not have tears on her face at all, nor would she stand there with her hands clasped upon her hips, so tightly and defiantly that, on the few times that I had seen her with such a pose (all of them on nights such as these, when my father's arrival would awaken me and bring me just outside the living room door, where I listened and watched as my parents threw words and other items at each other, seemingly unaware of the little minds and hearts that could be listening to them), I wondered if she would ever be able to move her hands again. No, my mother would be smiling, for it would not be the early morning hours of night at all. The dusk may have barely touched the night sky, and my father would then spend the whole night at home with us, his family. In my version of the story, he would be happy there and would never want to leave.

There came a time that summer, after my mother's death, when he and I had worked clearing the land, and the money we made was not enough. I said to my father, "I believe I may have to borrow money to survive this summer, until I get back to school in the fall." I asked if he would help, if need be, since I was not known in these parts anymore and so many of the local financial firms loaned money on a facial-recognition basis. He answered that he would have to see. His baby child would probably need his help as well, and he would have to take care of her first. I remember standing there by the truck, for he and I had quit working for the day and were getting a cool drink of water before we headed home. My mind truly stopped for some seconds. My mouth may have fell open, the bottom lip exposing the tender parts of my teeth. My eyes did move. They followed my father as he continued about his business, as though nothing had changed between us. He did not look at me, once, but I understood this to be "his way." I eventually looked away myself, and said, simply, "Okay."

As I write this now, I am not bitter—for I never did get his help, and I almost didn't survive financially that summer. Today, my heart aches in a different way. If tears fall (and they usually do), they come because I know that I will never work so closely with my father again, that our days as father and daughter, sharing the simple joys of nature and working with our hands, have come and gone. Wouldn't it be silly to lament his loss and only think of the things he did not give me, or did not help me with, or did not wish to share with me? Wouldn't it?

A man who has lived with cancer for over 16 years, longs to think that he will continue to live with it, for perhaps 16 more years, or even beyond. He, perhaps, begins to think that he can live with it forever.

At many church services, my father would stand in the pulpit and give testimony that sounded as though he were bragging about being alive. It always reminded me of people who did not understand the whole idea behind uncouthness. Like a woman who might remind everyone that her baked pies were better than another woman's, right to the woman's face.

"How uncouth," someone might then say.

"Just wasn't raised right," another might say.

"Don't need to brag about it," yet another might say.

"Some things, you just don't say," all would agree.

My father bragged about how the Lord had saved him: "The doctor's said I only had a year to live, and here I am, done lived many more. I am eight-tee eight years old. [And to this many in the congregation would marvel, for he looked much younger, got around like a man in his fifties, barely had gray hairs on his head and then only a few around his temples.] My chullin done planned a BIG celebration for my 90th birthday. Yes, Lord, you been good to me. I could' a been dead, sleeping in my grave, Lord, but you gave me another day."

Yes, this was his testimony, but he never thought about the people who hadn't been so blessed—those in the congregation who were ailing (many near their last breaths), those who had suffered greatly just to get themselves to church that day. Or those who had recently lost family members whose cancer took them early—only months after diagnosis, and not "oh, so many years" later. My father's lasting, his living well beyond the usual years, spurred him onward on these occasions and emboldened him to speak thusly on future opportunities. I knew he felt powerful and just. He took on the look of a man who knew things, who sat with knowledge tucked away, just beyond his coat jacket, in a pocket that no one could see.

On those church Sundays, when he stood before us, he imparted little bits of that knowledge, and the church members smiled and laughed with him, but I always thought some were false smiles. I wondered if, secretly, some of these church members were cursing my father beneath their breaths, softly crying out to God, saying, "Why not me, Lord?" I wondered if the witty little stories my father told were his way of assuaging their disdain of him, for having lived so long, when so many of them, much younger, had family members already passed on or would soon be gone themselves. I often sat there, wondered about these things, and told myself that I would mention these things to my father when later we spoke.

Over the years, I came to think of myself as the one who understood him, who knew him like none of my siblings did. This may not have been true, but this is how I came to feel. Early in his treatment, while I was still in college, working on my bachelor's degree, I would drive out, to the tiny community where I had grown up, to pick up my father and bring him to the VA Hospital in New Orleans. My sports car was little more than a two-seater, which meant that only my father could come; which meant that even my mother, who went everywhere with my father, could not squeeze into the car with us. What am I saying? She always had a smile on her face as she stood at the front door and waved us off; perhaps she knew that this was time my father and I wanted to spend with each other.

After we had finished for the day, after my father and I had maneuvered through the maze of patients and the seemingly nonsensical order of the appointment times and rituals, we would then leave the hospital and search for a great place to eat before we made our way home again. Most days, after we had eaten, we would spend hours at the table, talking about our present and past lives and all the things we might have changed along the way.

On the first of many of those days when my father and I sat talking, he asked me to write his life story. I laughed nervously at first, and said, "What? What would I write? I don't know what I would say, Daddy." This is when my father began to tell me the specifics of his life before I knew him. He told me all the details of having fought in World War II. He told me about his first wife and how he had come home from the war and found her shacked up with another man. He told me about his disappointment and about subsequently finding my mother, who was much younger than he was, but she was the best decision he had ever made. He told me about his early love for her and how tightly he had held her on that first date when he had double-dated with his brother and his girlfriend, and how all four of them had squeezed into the cab of his brother's truck.

After a while, I noticed that my father, like most people, mostly shared the good parts of his life story. In the back of my mind, I kept waiting for him to tell me why he had cheated on my mother, on our whole family. I wanted, for instance, him to tell me why, when we were children, he had been sleeping with the woman next door. I wanted to know why he had treated my sister Willie Vern, his stepdaughter, in an immoral way. I wanted to know why, back then, he had spent so much time away from our house and why he could never come home before the wee hours of the morning. I refused to write down anything that he told me, for none of it mattered to me. My ears dispelled everything that was not these truths. Yet my father kept talking, kept telling me the same stories over and over again.

It seems that when we get older, only the significant stories remain in our minds: the ones that represent the life-changing moments of our lives.

Everything else drops off from our memories and falls into that bottomless cavern of our minds, where few things are ever recovered. My father, no matter how many times we sat down to eat, would tell me the story of how terrible he had been as a child.

"I just had the devil in me," he'd say. "Couldn't help myself. I wanted mama and papa to beat it out of me. I could always find a way to get a whuppin."

He would often lie awake at night and listen to a familiar conversation his parents had, about him.

"What we gonna do about him?" his mother would ask.

"I'm gonna kill him, that's what I'm a do," his father would answer.

My father said he would smile to himself from on the other side of the wall, completely satisfied, and lost in this imperfect way of behavior—the only way he knew to get his parents' attention.

On a certain day in his childhood, my father had taken a hoe and "cocked" his little sister, Marie, "upside the head" with it. His father had then taken a leather strap to him and beat him all over his head and body. My father said his lips were so swollen that the only way he could eat was to physically pull his bottom lip open and shovel the food in. He assured me that his swollen lips remained that way for some time, and that once they had healed, he found new ways to incur his parents' beatings.

After I had heard my father tell me that story for about the hundredth time, I began to understand its significance—the reason why, of all the childhood stories he could tell, this one sat, in the later years of his life, upon his mind, and came to represent who he had become as a person. On one of those days, as I sat listening to him tell that story yet again, I said to myself, "When was it, Daddy, that they first told you that you were a bad person, that you were less than a person, and that you did not deserve all the good things in life?" And why had my father believed them? Sitting across the table from him, I could see that he had fully embraced this label he had been given as a young black male growing up during the depression, whose only value in life would be to work the cotton fields and to plow the hundreds of rows of vegetables, with the old mule from out back. I saw that my father had not been expected to "become" anyone or to "do anything" with his life. It was much later in life, perhaps on one of those days when he and I sat talking, that he himself came to realize his parents had beat him because they did not want the rest of the world to beat him more—or worse, to kill him.

As a young boy, teenager, and later a young man, he had clearly embraced the label. The world would not be nice and perfect for him. He accepted his consignation as though a good host had asked him to sit down at the table where his place setting for life had been prepared. This label became a tag—like those kinds that you wear at a big conference, where you pull the paper off the back and then stick it to the left side of your chest, so that everyone who then encounters you will know who you are. My father had worn his label every day of his life, and the world had known instantly who he was, without ever having to get to know him. On those lunch talks with my father, I saw that they had labeled him early—long before he arrived anywhere in life—and that he had never recovered from it.

A child can be so forgiving, and yet, she cannot see inside a father's heart. The only thing that she can see, clearly, is that her father, though he is handsome and funny and generous, is also hurting her mother. That he is hurting her mother. That he is hurting her mother, whom the child loves and appreciates more than the father because the mother is always there to take care of her. The child doesn't know it, but the mother, as a child, was never told that she was a bad person. The mother was born of a different time. And she was the baby girl child of her family, which means she was loved unconditionally, specially. A child does not see these things though. A child grows up disliking a father, the same one that she secretly wants to adore, and still blames him for all the bad things she saw in her young life, with her own eyes.

When I finally arrived at the hospital, after my father's operation, I sidled up to his hospital bed, and could see right off that he had changed. He was quiet, much quieter than usual. I couldn't imagine why. I finally surmised (or more likely, appeased myself with the idea) that he was still recovering from the surgery and just wasn't himself. Over the next days and weeks, his spirit returned somewhat, but every time I looked into his eyes, I could see that he was no longer satisfied with life. He asked me if I would stay with him and help him recover. I was on holiday break, which meant that I could not say, "No, Daddy, I have to work," or "No, I have to get back to the city" (to do some unspecified thing that could not be done at any other unspecified time).

What I truly wanted to say was, "No, Daddy, this is the first chance I've had to remain at home and get some writing done." In the weeks leading up to the holidays, I had literally dreamed of the free days that would be available to me. Free days to write. I had counted those days in my mind. I had told my family and friends that I would not be available to spend time with them. I had smiled gleefully just thinking about the days that I would spend waking up in the late afternoons (because I would have spent the entire night at the computer, allowing the words to completely fall out of me and onto the pages). Reader, you must understand that I had dreamed of these days of solitude, just as a young ballerina might dream of waking up one day and placing her feet down for a perfect pirouette, or a racer might dream of crossing the finishing line for the first time in his career. I had recently graduated (and received my MFA), and my mind was focused on no other thing past writing. These were going to be the days that would push me to the next level of my craft.

And yet, I said "Yes," to my father. Yes, to taking care of him, to coming home to live in the F.E.M.A. trailer with him, to cooking for him, to helping him clean himself, to reminding him of his doctor's orders, to traveling back and forth to the VA hospital with him for his sometimes daily appointments.

They say that when cancer patients realize the end is near, they look for even the smallest of ways to maintain some type of control of their lives. The many trips that my father and I took to the VA hospital were like moments of freedom for him. Perhaps the time that he and I shared had come to represent a type of autonomy that he had found with self: a time to get away from his everyday life and commune with someone who had the semblance of understanding who he was in those final months of his life.

Though my father smiled, there was a type of sadness that overtook him daily. I would not allow myself to think the obvious: that he was dying for certain, just not as slowly as he had been since his original diagnosis. During those days, weeks, that I spent with him over the holidays, it seemed to both of us that we had beaten the odds again, and that he would recover fully from the surgery. He already spoke of planting his garden, as soon as the weather was warm enough.

"Some butter beans and okra," he joked, knowing that my face would light up, my soul really, for those were the foods that my mother had always prepared especially for me, foods that I loved religiously.

There were also days when he was anxious and his voice more caustic, bitter. On one morning, as I helped him prepare for the day's journey to the VA, his bowels moved faster than we could make the short steps to the bathroom. The diaper that he wore had been too loosely fitted, and much of the excrement went straining down his legs.

I had noticed a strange thing about my father over these weeks: he no longer cared much for modesty or decorum. "I'm not your son," I found myself saying once or twice. "These are things I should not be seeing." He admonished it away, saying, "Just help me, will you?" He said these words in the same tone with which he often chastised one of my sisters who had gotten so big that my father would at times, sit across from her at dinner and tell her how fat she was. In those moments, I would remember all the stored up rage I felt for him. Who talked to their child this way? I had always hated this idea of favorites (my mother had gotten over her special love for my brother Lionel many years before, but my father seemed to think it was okay to treat some of his children differently than he did others). I simply hated this piece of his character.

Sometimes, when it was just him and me in the F.E.M.A. trailer, he would talk about the people (mostly his children) who had fallen short in their lives, and I would think to myself, "Surely, father, you can't see their faults more clearly than your own!" And I would make excuses for these people (mostly his children) and would say to him that these people hadn't always had an easy path in their lives. And I would point out the one fact that would settle his sudden ire: how some of his children had grown up in a house that was not fit to live in, that they had still been living in when Katrina hit, and mostly because he never saw the need to provide accommodations that were better. Our conversations would lag then, and the air would grow heavier.

After a few moments, my father would say, "I sure hope I can plant some butter beans and okra this year."

Months later, when I had gone back to work, when either my sister Venesta or I were tasked with driving my father to the VA for his almost daily appointments, I saw, in miniscule moments, pieces of my father that I had never seen before.

"Pull up to the door," he'd say. "Let me out, and you go park the car."

After I had driven off, I would look for him in the rear view mirror. He would wait for one of the wheelchair assistants to come and offer him a ride. Rarely would he still be sitting there when I returned. Later, when I had caught up with him in whatever office his appointment was scheduled, he would bark instructions at me, and if I did not go in the direction he wanted or did not stop when he asked or did not go to the pharmacy instead of the waiting room, or any other thing he wanted, he might yell out, uncharacteristically, "Stop, Girl, Ness, Lu. Do what I tell you!" (In the last days, he rarely placed the correct name with the correct child.)

These snaps in his personality did not happen often, but when they did, I jumped in fear, and I pushed my father a little faster, in whatever direction he chose.

Our conversations were beginning to stop.

On one visit, I wheeled my father into a chemotherapist's office. The young Japanese American doctor, handsome and tall and friendly, stood bent over, just in front of my father, with one of his feet on a stool and his elbow on his knee, and said to my father, "There's no use trying it. You have too many other complications, with your heart and your leg." (My father had been shot in his leg in the Army and had reinjured it in a tractor accident many years later.)

My father smiled, in an almost refined way, and said, "So, that's it? What else can you do for me?"

The young doctor did not know what to say, other than, "We'll make an appointment, so you can talk with your primary doctor."

I did not get the impression that either my father or I understood, specifically, that this meant, THERE IS NO HOPE. I did not surmise that this was a statement by a doctor, saying that my father's cancer had spread to the point of no return. He had lasted so long with the disease that we all apparently thought that he could go on and on, forever.

And, over the next months, as if my father wanted to prove the young doctor wrong, he improved drastically. He literally got up from his sick bed and seemed more like himself. He was even driving himself to church in his old raggedy car. He planted that garden, with greens and corn, and of course, butter beans and okra. When I called home, he continued to make jokes the way he always did. Before I'd get off the phone, he would make sure all his children were coming to church services on Sunday. He didn't want to hear about gas prices that were high, or that my sister and I could not afford to make the trip home so often. He only wanted to see our faces. There was a sense of urgency there, yet I did not see it. Even with the next two hospitalizations, none of us saw that he was at the very end of his life. We never stopped to think that the end was so near.

One thing that many people did not see is that my father was a suffering man. Not strictly physically, I mean. His heart was actually aching. On some days as we drove to Jackson, where he was being treated since Katrina, he told me of a plan he had to get a new house for his children who still needed to live there. This was weighing on his mind, he said. I could see that it was one more thing that he felt responsible for getting right before he died. My mind went back to the first days of his diagnosis, when he had promised my mother that he would be a better husband, when he had cooked for her and waited on her as though she were royalty. I saw him trying to make up for all the days when he had not gotten it right. He had become a minister and had begun to stand up in the pulpit and proclaim his love for God. He had begun a prison ministry, hoping to save more lost souls and bring them to Christ. He had spent days and nights trying to change two of his sons, both of whom had followed in his footsteps, by chasing women and beer.

"I was wrong," he often said to them, "And so are you." Sure, he never addressed the little pinches and feels that he gave our half-sister Willie, when presumably no one was looking, nor what his oldest sons may have learned from watching his behavior. None of it was his fault; he just wanted them to be better than he was. How could I explain how impossible that had been; his two oldest boys (the ones who grew up watching his immoral behavior) had learned to act in a similar way, and we (Venesta and I) were the girls who had to consistently and repulsively push them away. I think about it years later, long after he has gone, and I realize that he did see, just that. He saw it quite clearly; so much so that it was eating him up inside. He just didn't know how to say how sorry he was. In those last days, he did what he thought was best to make things right.

In seventeen years, my father had changed all the big faults, the chinks in his armor that had been obvious to see. It was as though he had looked into his after life and was able to see the ugly truths of his past. And on those days, when he stood in the pulpit and bragged about how great God had been to him, he wasn't bragging at all. He understood that not all those other people needed as much time to correct the mistakes of their lives. He was still vigorously trying to correct the obvious sins. Everything else would have to wait.

A DAUGHTER REMEMBERS... HER FATHER

My father chose my mother's birthday to die on. As the date approached, I had no idea that such a thing would happen. I had listened to the doctors say, "It could be days, weeks." I had stood in the emergency room, on his final hospital visit, and watched my father's face go blank when a strong, yet kindly doctor had said to him, "The cancer has spread, Mr. James, but I'm sure you already know this." I watched my father look over to me and leave his eyes there because he didn't know what else to do or say perhaps. Or was it because he felt guilty? Hadn't he insisted on dragging us to yet another hospital, just to hear them say what he had apparently already been told? I wanted to hate him for not telling me. But then I thought back to that day when the young Japanese American doctor had said similar words. None of us had wanted to face the truth. It was easier to think that he would just go on living, no matter how sickly be became.

This emergency room doctor insisted that I ask the right questions, to be sure. He looked at us as though we were crazy people—how could we come to the emergency room expecting a miracle, when my father's insides were so eaten up with cancer. "A new cancer, to be sure," he said. At last, I found out that the old prostate cancer was still running its course, had never really moved much. This new cancer had spread from his stomach into his lymph nodes and liver and so many other places.

The doctors allowed my father to remain there in a hospital that was not the VA, for it was the humane thing to do. "They done give up on me," he said, speaking of his hearty yet temperamental doctors at the VA.

My father left the emergency room, and tests were done on his stomach, just to be sure nothing could be done. Perhaps, we all thought, they can find an opening, or loophole, so that he can eat and digest his food. Nothing of the sort happened. And then a week, then another, passed, and the doctors sent him home to die.

There were so many in my family who were not prepared for his demise. My baby sister seemed to refuse to accept the fact that he was headed for the next life, at least that was the impression I got. I found myself saying to her, "Face the truth, your father is dying." I then found myself crying, for many nights, because even though I had accepted the inevitability of it all, I still wondered why I hadn't seen it coming—me, who had spent so much time with him in those waning days.

Only recently have I realized that he never wanted us to know how close he was to death. After all, he had not spent his life lamenting our feelings about him. How fitting that he would watch over us during these last, most difficult times of his life. As for me, well, I simply could not have carried on knowing that I was about to lose my father.

The Woodpecker

My father's eyes are always open, or they blink to his rhythm in nature. In a gown he has worn home from the hospital, he sits at the edge of the bed, soaked to his bottom, unable to go to the bathroom properly, on his own. His diaper needs to be changed.

"My dyddie is wet," he says, unashamed and with a smile. He has not lost his cool, irreverent sense of humor.

He has boys' eyes—eyes that wish to see where he will be going. He is holding on, I know, with all his strength. He wants to reach ninety, just half a year away.

"Oh, the party my girls'll give me," he says, and it is as clear as anything to be imagined: he will make it. Screw those doctors, what do they know?

He waits for me to come to him, to cross the small room of the Katrina trailer. I have been sitting at the table still eating my breakfast. I cannot help but see him as he is: aren't those his toes beginning to curl, signaling the end of his long and passionate life? But optimism flitters all around him, pecking at his heart. Ah, the sound of it.

He listens . . . tap, tap, tap, tap, tap.

The woodpecker is no more than thirty feet outside the window. It hangs, by its claws, from a broken hickory tree that has its top missing. I am sure the tree was healthy in its youth, and grew even stronger against the uncooperativeness of time. But then it grew old, or wasn't properly nourished, which left it vulnerable to a most obtrusive wind.

The bird's color is there—a full red slice down its small crown, which makes it male. The wings are black and white ridges, with a splash of red, barely visible on the bird's tummy. My father and I have spent many moments aching over the bird's red-bellied beauty.

"Remember the one we used to have in the yard?" I ask him. That was at our first house, all those years ago. As a young girl, I would sit in the grass and wait for the giant woodpecker—a full red head and impressive black wings.

After we've listened for a long while, my father says, "Yeah, but this one's better." The bird, it moves in circles around the old tree . . . tap, tap, tap, tap, tap. I imagine the sound reminds my father of the weapons he used in war, or the sound of the gunfire from a distance . . . tap, tap, tap, tap, tap.

My father and I have history. We are both people of nature. We tried to save an ailing chicken hawk one summer—the bird, in its final hours, searched my father and me out as we cleared away weeds from beneath fine oak trees, which simply wanted to grow freely and give off an air of greatness and indignation. We found the bird waiting near our truck and later took it to the nearest vet clinic. But we were too late.

We used to ride in my sports car, with the windows down, as we crossed the Causeway, from the country to New Orleans, or to Jackson and back, rushing to his doctors' visits. We were both troubled by the VA: he, the real soldier, having fought for his country in World War II; and me, who served the navy well as a yeoman, but never pointed a rifle at another soul. On the car rides home, we'd complain about the state of the VA hospitals and how carelessly they sometimes treated the vets.

Often we'd stop at diners, and he'd tell me his life's stories, once again, sure that one day I would write them down. The stories never changed but remained planted, like small trees, growing in my memory. How he got shot in the leg in the Aleutians. How he came home from the military and found his first wife "shacked up" with another man. How he married my mother on Valentine's Day. How sorry he was to have mistreated her over the years of their marriage.

We'd sit in old booths and eat omelets, and he'd smile, as though he were lighter, having spoken his truth once more—neither of us aware of how quickly those moments were passing.

When I go to him, and help him up from the bed, I feel guilty—mostly for blaming him for so long. Perhaps the blame shifted to guilt. It could be why I am here now, doing all the dirty work.

Slowly, he leans his bent, frail body into mine. He has the walk of a baby bird. His feet, a slight rhythm, a sure tap here and then there—not steady like music, or the tick of a clock. But it's his rhythm. We near the bathroom, and he slows even more.

We both hear the tap, tap, tap, tap, tap, so close beyond the window.

Reader's Guide and Discussion Questions for *Table Scraps and Other Essays*

- **Nature**—Writers such as Henry David Thoreau (in Walden) remind us of the close relationship we humans have with nature. The essay "On Becoming a Naturalist" suggests James feels more at home in the outdoors, and explains why she came to rely on nature as a comforting force during the most difficult times of her childhood. James says, "I was naturally attracted to the outdoors"; her "early escapades with nature" are what solidified her status as a naturalist. Do you believe her family's devotion to the land is what nurtured these instincts?
- **Symbolism**—Discuss the symbols of the titled essays, "The River," "The Chicken Hawk," "The Woodpecker," as well as "The Guardian." Beyond the literal level, such titles suggest the essays might be read on a figurative level as well. Reread these essays, but spend a few minutes exploring the titles, looking for both connotative and denotative meanings of "river," "chicken and hawk", "woodpecker," and "guardian." Note how these terms might be read symbolically and offer a deeper meaning to each essay. What is the significance of birds in James's essays?
- **Language**—James's writing has often been called "beautiful, lyrical, and appealing." Discuss specific essays or sections of the collection that appeal to your senses most. To what do you attribute the rich

imagery of James's writing style? The essay, "Daddy, It's Your Child Song," for example, uses imagery so distinct that the reader is able to sense the beauty of the land that James is describing. Can you note other examples of rich, powerful imagery in James's writing?

- **Father/daughter relationship**—Discuss the essays that reveal the father/daughter relationship most. What type of relationship does James have with her father: as a child, a young adult, and an adult who must care for her father in his declining years? How does James learn to forgive her father toward the latter years of their relationship? Clearly, the father's recognition of his mortality helps him change and become the man, husband, father his family has needed. Do you think the father is actually able to forgive himself?

- **Forgiveness**—In the Foreword to the collection, Randy Bates notes how James's Christian ideals and values affect the woman she becomes later in life. Discuss the overwhelming presence of religion, as seen in "Piece of a Tree," for example. Does James's Christian background help her in understanding the value of forgiveness? Think about your own personal stories and note the times you were able to either grant forgiveness (or not) to others.

- **Mother/daughter relationship**—Discuss the mother overall and her impact on James's young life. If the mother is a steadying force, what lessons does James learn from her mother? Do you think the mother's longsuffering attitude and her faith in God are inspiring to James? If not, why not? What types of qualities (good or bad) do you think the mother has passed on to James, and possibly her siblings?

- **Theme**—why do you think the mother in James's essays does not leave her philandering, abusive husband at some point in their embattled relationship? Why does the mother insist on encouraging a respectful relationship between the children and their father? Is it significant that the mother dies before the father? In "A Daughter Remembers," James says she and her father would spend precious days together, with her driving him to his doctors' appointments. How does this individual time that James spends with her father help change her negative view of him?

- **Education**—Discuss the importance of education in the essays overall, but particularly in "The Guardian" and "Pieces of a Tree." Discuss the impact that teachers like Mrs. Hart and Mrs. Cornist have on

READER'S GUIDE AND DISCUSSION QUESTIONS

James as a young female child. How might these teachers have influenced who James became as an adult? Name other types of influences that you see in the essays.

- **Race**—Discuss the seemingly non-issue of race in a collection about an African American female growing up in the Deep South. What is the relationship between the whites and blacks in James's childhood? Why does the concept of race get pushed into the background of most of these essays? What, then, becomes a prevailing theme(s), and are therefore of more importance, to this black family?

- **Death in Memoir**—Many memoir writers write about the theme of death. Terry Tempest Williams, for example, offers *Refuge: An Unnatural History of Family and Place*, in which she describes the difficult days of letting go of her dying mother, while noting an incredible empathy for the plight of the birds that inhabit the bear River Migratory Bird Refuge. In what ways does James, subtly or otherwise, address the subject of death in writing about her mother, in "Momma," her father, in "A Daughter Remembers," her sister, in "Willie Vern," and her teacher, in "The Guardian"?

- **Memory**—James has often said that there is "beauty in memory." What do you think she means by this, especially in writing essays, which require the most exact memory. An example is "My Brother Went Down," where James must accurately describe the detailed moments of the fear she felt during a baptism at a local creek. You might discuss the collection overall as memoir writing and what role memory plays in writing memoir.

- **Katrina**—Discuss the essays in which James reflects on the Katrina disaster; namely, "Living Spaces" and "As Fortunes Go." Note the differences in theme, location, and style of these two essays. Both are written in the style of lyric essays. How do these essays fit into the collection? What are the most salient (obvious) lessons to be learned from this moment in history, as seen from James's perspective?

- **Structure**—Note the varying structure of the essays in the collection. What is the purpose, for example, of smaller essays such as "Sugar Cane" and "Old Man Carves an Ax Handle"? Reread "Momma" and answer how does an essay written in verse fit into a collection of prose essays? What do you think James accomplishes with this unpredictable style of writing?

READER'S GUIDE AND DISCUSSION QUESTIONS

- **Beginning, Middle, and End**. Aristotle said the best writing has a clear beginning, middle, and end. Discuss the opening and closing essays, "Table Scraps" and "The Woodpecker," and how each sets up or resolves many of the themes that are reflected in the collection. Has James succeeded in offering strong and connective essays that ultimately tell a cohesive story?

- **Writer as Self**—discuss the collection from the author's perspective, as a writer writing her true-life stories. What are some of the literary conventions this writer might have drawn upon when writing from a writer's perspective.

Bibliography

Anonymous, "Let Us Go Down to Jordan."
Anonymous, "I Have Decided To Follow Jesus."
Anonymous, "Lord, I Want to Be a Christian."
Anonymous, "I Shall Not Be Moved." Public Domain (1929).
Boccaccio, Giovanni. The Project Gutenberg eBook of *The Decameron*, 1353. Retrieved from www.gutenberg.org/files/23700/23700-h/23700-h.htm
Boethius, Anicius Manlius Severinus. *The Consolation of Philosophy*, trans. W. V. Cooper, book II, pr. 4, L. ii. London: J.M. Dent Co., 1902.
Covay, Don. "Chain of Fools." Aretha Franklin, *Lady Soul*, November 1967, Atlantic Records, Producer, Jerry Wexler.
Emerson, Ralph Waldo. *Nature*: "Chapter 1; p. 2" (1836). Retrieved from https://emersoncentral.com/ebook/Nature.pdf
Gaines, Ernest J. "Just Like a Tree." *The Sewanee Review* 71, no. 4 (Autumn, 1963): 567.
Gardner, Howard. "A Rounded Version: The Theory of Multiple Intelligences." *New Horizons in Theory and Practice*. Basic Books, Reprint Edition, 2006.
Kafka, Franz. *The Diaries of Franz Kafka*, 1910-1913. Retrieved from archive.org/details/in.ernet.dli.2015.499492/page/n5
Kierkegaard, Soren. *Journals: Search for Personal Meaning*, 1830s.
Millay, Edna St. Vincent. "Spring." *Second April*. New York: Mitchell Kennerley, 1921. 1.
Plato. *The Republic*, "Book 3." Project Guttenberg, trans. Benjamin Jowett. Retrieved from https://www.gutenberg.org/files/1497/1497-h/1497-h.htm
Plato. *The Republic*, "Book 3." The University of Adelaide, trans. Benjamin Jowett. Retrieved from https://ebooks.adelaide.edu.au/p/plato/p71r/book03.html
Plato, *Symposium*, trans. W. Hamilton, 87. Penguin Classics, 1956.
Wesley, Charles. "Father I Stretch My Hands to Thee" *The Africana Hymnal*.